A THEOLOGY OF CARNIVAL AND OTHER PROVOCATIONS

The Reverend Clifford Rawlins

Copyright © 2021 The Reverend Clifford Rawlins

All rights reserved. No part of this book may be reproduced, stored, or transmitted by any means—whether auditory, graphic, mechanical, or electronic—without written permission of both publisher and author, except in the case of brief excerpts used in critical articles and reviews. Unauthorized reproduction of any part of this work is illegal and is punishable by law.

To contact the publisher please visit our website.
www.trinityhillspublishing.com
92 Cipero Road
Retrench Village
SanFernando
Trinidad and Tobago

PREFACE

The word 'provoke' comes from two Latin words, pro vocare, meaning literally to call forth. These essays seek to do just that in relation to a Caribbean theology which has grown virtually dormant, complacent and for all intents and purposes taken over by a North American brand of fundamentalist evangelicalism. This work seeks to stoke the embers of a complacent but latent Caribbean theology by provoking readers to think beyond the confines of a theology shaped by the colonial past and the North American tele-evangelist, mega church brand to call forth one that is relevant to the present age and landscape.

These essays are commended with prophetic grace and pilgrim quality that invite and engage readers to embark on a journey where we re-imagine God's work and will for a new people in a new era. A time such as this provides us with an opportunity to reflect. We must reflect on our theology. For instance, what is our theology of gender justice in the face of gender-based violence and the sexual abuse of children that pervade our society? How prophetic are we in today's changing world? Are we a radical voice for the marginalised? We must reflect on how we do theology, be honest in our interpretation of the Bible, and apply that interpretation to serve the present age, which is the only age we in our time are called to serve. Where are we coming from and where are we going? We will need to interrogate the Caribbean appropriation of sacred texts in Christianity, as well as the use of oral and colonial traditions to support views and mindsets that have shaped and dominated the landscape. Deconstruction and reinterpreting these texts to transform the local landscape must be undertaken in order to discover and deliver the justice and peace of God's Reign while acknowledging the positive resources from world religions. We need new eyes for seeing, new hands for holding on. "New occasions teach new duties, time makes ancient good uncouth, They must upward still and onward, who would keep abreast of truth." James Russell Lowell

A THEOLOGY OF CARNIVAL

Just mention the word, 'Carnival', and a host of negative comments ensue from puritan-minded churches and pastors relating to all the biblical vices of lust, lasciviousness, licentiousness, revelry, and debauchery. These are no doubt taken from the Pauline worldview of the then Roman Empire with its pagan rites of Bacchanalia, intended as actual worship of the god of wine, Bacchus. Many would agree with Reformed liturgical scholar, J.J.Von Allmen that Carnival in its very essence has not so much to do with culture as it has with pagan Roman religion and that the participant, unwittingly so, gives oneself over to the influence of demon spirits and influences. Von Allmen, surmises in his treatise on Reformed worship, *"Although Jesus Christ—since his triumph over them by the cross—holds in check the demons who have perverted the original cult to their own advantage—whether to assure their own glory or to obtain by this means control over mankind—these demons, powerless as they are, are not yet dead. To play with them, to make folk-lorist obeisances to them (as in the Carnival), to restore some of their lost prestige by taking them as mythological types symbolizing the life of men (as in the Festival of the Vinedressers), is to play too risky a game: not only because of the virulence of these demons, but because such manifestations arouse a longing for the time of 'Egyptian servitude' when surrender to Christ had not yet been made. It is not by chance that scripture likens the lapse into these cults as an act of adultery, and here again we must remember that some kinds of adultery can be consummated simply by a glance."* (1).

This outlook stems from the classic Augustinian worldview that divides the world into two sharply opposing and distinct ways of being; the sacred and the secular or sometimes, the profane; the Christian, refined and destined for eternal glory, and the non-

Christian, perverted and doomed. As Augustine himself would be accredited with saying, "Extra ecclesia nulla salus est." (Outside the Church, none is saved). Indeed Von Allmen concurs by saying, "*The [non-Christian cults] have therefore nothing to lose by self-renunciation, by consenting to die in Christ. What they have perverted will be reborn, will arise again in a purified state and their deep purpose, their appeal, their readiness to give themselves, their summons to the materials of the world that [they] might be made to serve art and culture—all that, cleansed, reborn, redirected, will be restored to them.*" (2). An argument such as this serves well the intentions of official Christian [Reformed] liturgy, and of one's renouncing former non-Christian ways upon becoming Christian. And whereas culture might be used to serve Christian liturgy, the problem lies in an attempt to Christianise culture in totality, under the intention of seeking to claim the overlordship of Christ over everything. And therefore the only kind of culture that would be valid would be one that serves the Christian cult.

Previously this was thought of as imposing European culture over conquered non-European ones in an imperialist age. Is it that any and everything outside of the Judaeo—Christian deposit is demonic and invalid and thus needs to be 'baptised' and attributed to the Christian God? There are people who will listen to none other than gospel music, because other types are demon-influenced and things of the world. Can it be that becoming drunk and staggering in the streets for the feast of Purim, celebrating Jewish liberation from possible genocide through a Persian official [see the book of Esther], is right, but getting drunk generally is wrong? Or can it be that David's half-naked dancing, wining and gyrating in the streets to celebrate the triumphant recapture of the Ark of the Covenant from the Philistines is good because he, 'danced before the Lord', his wife's disdain of it, wrong, 2 Sam. 6:14 and, the otherwise dancing, wining and gyrating on nationally appointed days of jubilation is wrong because it is not, 'before the Lord' per se, and other's disdain of the latter is then correct and approving? No small wonder that Pentecostalist type churches are approving of such music, dancing and other physical movements in their worship, which very said, exact, same thing, if found in an ultra-Christian or even ultra-religious context, would be condemned as revelry and bacchanal. Culture, though, is a liturgy all its own, remembering that liturgy comes from the Koine Greek for 'public work'. It manifests itself as a separate and distinct gift of God for the expression of worship in ultra-religious words and forms and of God's goodness in creation and faithfulness to it. And the same questions that are asked of the ordering of family life and social relationships within the context of the new and redeemed humanity brought about in Jesus Christ, must be asked of the culture here, for culture is the soul of the community, its uniting force and the expression of its being.

There is also the need to acknowledge that the gospel transcends all cultures and that in any event, all cultures need the gospel. The prophetic grace of the gospel must also be allowed to critique and baptise the culture and local landscape, thus bringing it into the new and redeemed order of creation; through identification with the person and work of Christ, by removing those things that are foreign to justice, joy, mutual edification, compassion, peace, beauty and order. In his incarnation, he is the Word made Flesh and dwelling among us, not in some far off distant land and in another time and era. In his resurrection and ascension he becomes the cosmic overlord who is bringing all creation to the fulness of its destiny. To validly critique the culture, the Reformed Tradition in particular and the Christian church as a whole, need to see the world as a created whole and not in its traditional Augustinian worldview of biblically sacred and secularly profane and devil-inspired after the Fall. An ancient Eucharistic liturgy symbolises this dynamic relationship between the death of Christ that brings forth new life and the creative forces of both nature and humanity;

> *"Blessed are you, Lord, God of all creation.*
> *Through your goodness we have this bread to offer,*
> *Which earth has given and human hands have made.*
> *It will become for us the bread of life.*
> *Blessed be God for ever.*

Blessed are you, Lord, God of all creation.
Through your goodness we have this wine to offer,
Fruit of the vine and work of human hands.
It will become for us the cup of salvation.

Blessed are you, Lord, God of all creation.
Through your goodness we have ourselves to offer,
Fruit of the womb, and formed by your love.
We will become your people for the world.
Blessed be God for ever." (3).

The prayer also implies that what is being offered is not just the actual bread, wine and people in the actual moment, but they are given as representations of the sum total of all created existence; human, natural and metaphysical: the energies of life, the struggles, being ground and crushed, burnt and bruised like wheat and grape to make bread and wine. It symbolises all of life as a search for wholeness. People desire to be fully human, with dis-ease and disappointment as well as strength and accomplishment, and be thus fully present with God and presented to God, who himself is fully present with his creation in Christ Jesus and who alone can make perfect the offering.

Carnival in Trinidad and Tobago can claim two distinct fountains of origin; the more noticeable being the Latinised European i.e. French and Spanish source, because of the time when it is celebrated, and the other being the African heritage because of the nature of many of the celebrations. In the former regard the festival was brought to these shores by the French settlers who came under the Cedula of Population of 1783 and lasted from Christmas to the Tuesday before Ash Wednesday, primarily as a festival of 'carne-vale' or 'farewell to the flesh' prior to the stringent fasts of Lent, but also on the new landscape it was beginning to take on a local validity because it was the driest and coolest time of the year when not much attention was needed agriculturally on the plantations and before the oncoming feverish activity of the cane cutting season (4). This season was marked with masked balls, soirees, dinner and garden parties, carolling from house to house and other occasions of gaiety and prankish behaviour. British culture, however, was more prone to celebrations at Christmas for the English and New Year's or Hogmanay for the Scots, which were seasons of excessive merrymaking. And in older British colonies the slaves were given freedom to engender their own festivities, as with the Jonkunno celebrations in the Bahamas, Jamaica and the northeastern Caribbean islands. In Barbados there has been the Kadooment or Cropover festival to mark the end of the sugarcane harvest with its origins from as early as c.1688. There had also been the concomitant imposition of martial law at these times to ensure the rule of law and order (5). Carnival celebrations among the former slave population in Trinidad only came into being with their emancipation in 1834, which they marked with great festivity. Selwyn Cudjoe remarks, *"Essentially, Carnival tried to recreate, reassemble and resurrect an African way of life that the colonial authorities attempted to stifle during slavery."* (6). Yet, there would be a deeper reactionary sentiment against a system in which they were unmistakably disempowered in every way. By 1844 these two festivals of the two main classes of society would be merged into one and limited to a two-day, pre-Lenten festival by the British, in an attempt to exercise a measure of control over the fomenting anti-British sentiment on the one hand by the French ascendancy and, anti-colonial feeling by the newly freed African population on the other.

The masses of newly freed peoples formed the substantive part of the society and the lower ranks at that. Even then, there would be two categories of lower class citizens. One made up of those who were only economically impoverished but who held on to values and mores derived from their religious traditions, Christian and / or otherwise and mainly rural; and the other, a mass of people who formed the underworld of brigands, prostitutes, bad johns, stickfighters and obeah men, which flouted sexuality and flirted with obscenity. The former would become characterised as the 'silent faithful' who, though recognising their unequal status in society, struggled inwardly through their prayers and concerns. The latter would be more bold and open in their challenge of the social conventions of the day, the protesters and rabble rousers who were braver in giving a voice to their silent compatriots. This latter group would come to dominate the Carnival celebrations and displace the provenance of French creole society. They would be given the name 'Jamette' society, from the French 'diametre', not only because their women and prostitutes would sensually show off their buxom waist diameters but chiefly because they were considered to fall below the diameter of respectable socially accepted behavioural standards. As calypsonian The Mighty Sparrow sings in his classic rendition of 'Slave',

> "*Times changed in so many ways,*
> *Till one day somebody say, 'Free de bloody slaves!'*
> *I was then put out on the street,*
> *I had no clothes, ah had no food, had no place to sleep.*
> *I had no education, no particular ambition,*
> *This I cannot conceal;*
> *Forgot my native culture,*
> *Ah had to live like a vulture;*
> *From the white man I had to steal."* (7)

Jamettised society, as Selwyn Cudjoe has come to describe it, can be seen today in the perpetuation of an undesirable underworld that has expanded to include trafficking in drugs and guns and the escalation of gang and turf warfare. The perception of being a 'bad john' has been transmuted from stickfighters to gunmen where the sentiments of the old songs are still aroused by the thirst for violence and blood; "Bois man nah fraid bois man," or still this classic chant sung in a call and response style, the first line being repeated as a response after every following statement,

> "*When ah dead, bury meh clothes,*
> *Ah doh want nobody to cry for me,*
> *Man, put everything in de cemetery,*
> *Ah doh want dem boys wear mih shirt and tie,*
> *And doh forget to tell meh mooma doh cry."* (8)

'Bois' being French for 'wood' or 'stick' and the stickfighter's virulence was seen in the size and strength of his wood, a play on his sexual abilities as well. The stick might also be infused with mystical properties through obeah of some kind to enhance its power. But stickfighting nonetheless had and still has an artform similar to that of sword fighting, or of the Oriental and African Martial Arts and in more recent times has been turned into a professional display of skill while still invoking the old haunts of 'bad johnism'.

This Jamette society took over Carnival and demonstrated an African way of life and being in their songs, dances, drumming, ritual, the use of masks, in the poetry of Pierrot Grenade and the Midnight Robber. Cudjoe concurs, "*Trinidad Carnival, however, was not merely a caricature of white society or the mere transformation of the French mardi gras. In the hands of Africans, Carnival turned out to be a stage where many talents were fused together, and turned into a springboard for exploring cultural heritage.*" (9). But they also incarnated their struggles in their portrayals, even as God became incarnate among his people in solidarity with human pain and suffering and struggles against imperial domination and an unequal society. Their devils or 'jab jab' from the French 'diable' portrayed the economic hell of deplorable living and working conditions, a people without moral direction as they were not good enough to go to church. The 'jab molasie' or molasses devil with his cracking whips and enchained body, and breathing fire and demanding money from bystanders, showed the cruel and demonic nature of the sugar industry (from which molasses is derived) that held them captive for so many years and deprived them of basic human dignity. These were not devil worshippers as vitriolic preachers would condemn. It was the devil of slavery, the sugarcane devil, the whip of the slave master. The devil, therefore, becomes a metaphor for social evil. Their baby doll and pregnant women costumes gave light to the plight of unwed and / or teenage mothers without any paternal support from their male 'saga boy' partners, nowadays glorified as 'players'. There was a subliminal aggression against the traces of empire found within the society that gave rise to a preponderance of stickfighting, whips, chains, threatening verbose speeches, and extortion of money from the public. The anti-heroes of western culture were celebrated, Native American Indians, robbers, devils and imps, vampires and bats. The Midnight Robber with his grandiose claims to greatness and an ancestral lineage of the world's greatest fiends becomes a modern day Robin Hood who takes back from the rich what they have stolen and restores them to the original poorer class owners. The pretensions of respectable society were burlesqued in the Dame Lorraine skit, and in the satire and picong of calypso (10). These constituted part of the early democratic institutions of the emerging society. There were always imperialist attempts to restrict the new found expressions of the people out of fear that the freedom of expression, speech and movement might destabilize colonial rule and ascendancy but also because the colonial society was able to see the hypocrisy of its pretensions unmasked in the masks of the revellers, and seeing themselves for who they really were, they felt all the more threatened. This was truly street theatre at its best; the word hypocrite in Koine Greek originally meant 'to judge over the mask' and was the common word to describe an actor.

The book, 'Trinidad Carnival' notes, *"But carnival in Trinidad, like similar festivals throughout the Caribbean, had become a focal point for the elaboration of African cultural retentions in music, dance, costume and ritual, and a celebration of freedom. Attempts to even restrict it were bitterly fought by lower class mobs and a few middle class black nationalists, and things grew more rowdy as the century plunged into recession, swelling the urban slums with unemployed men and women, and the carnival, according to Pearse, with 'singers, drummers, dancers stickmen, prostitutes, matadors, bad-johns, dunois, makos (maquereau or pimp)* and corner boys, that is to say the 'jamette class,' and racial and political resentment boiled, between men and women, black and coloured, Roman Catholic and Anglican, creole and immigrant, but especially between the black lower class and the white upper class, all climaxing in the famous Canboulay Riots of the 1880's."* (11). To dismiss Trinidad and Tobago Carnival simply as pagan revelry is to miss entirely the point of a celebration that represents, in its fulness, the cleavings of a society in flux, the tensions and travails of an emerging people, who are yet to come into their own. Not to accept it is to miss the point of one's sense of being, one's sense of rootedness to the new place, of one's Trinidadianess or Tobagonianess. It would mean denying all that has made the peoples of this land who they are, and that has led the society to its present point in time.

This portrayal of society in all its cleavings, unmasked behind the masque or mas' as it has been adapted locally, reflects the fallenness of the human condition. It is a humanity unredeemed spiritually, morally and economically, in the fullest sense of the word as the Jamettised society did not have a place in the 'oikoumene', or the inhabited place, as Sparrow brings to mind,

> *"I was then put out on the street,*
> *I had no clothes, ah had no food, had no place to sleep.*
> *I had no education, no particular ambition,*
> *This I cannot conceal;*
> *Forgot my native culture,*
> *Ah had to live like a vulture..."* (12).

Puritannical Christianity: Roman, Reformed and Evangelical; have tended to look at the more obscene portrayals as repugnant to good behaviour. Masqueraders flaunted their sexuality openly, in what many would consider lewd and obscene, in a demonstration of female independence and male sexual machismo. Christianity condemns this in Carnival and perhaps rightly so when there is the tendency to go overboard with certain portrayals. Carnival is not just the incarnation of the struggles of the lower classes against the system in their portrayals, it is also a representation, an iconic image of the reality of such a Jamettised society. Therefore, in relation to the cosmic Christ it is both incarnation, as he who is God became human, and iconic in mirroring society's reality even as Christ is the image or icon of God, Colossians 1:15, Hebrews 1:3. Must the true nature of the society be hidden? Innocence does not preclude a removal of the evil, but the maintenance of self-restraint in the presence of it, as with the story of the serpent in a supposedly perfect environment of the Garden of Eden. If the good people remain by themselves, then how is the church supposed to be salt and light to the world, when the salt refuses to be mixed, or the light runs from the darkness? The demon must be named in order for it to be exorcised, especially the demons of an oppressive system manifested in the carnival portrayals, which demons deny a place in the oikoumene to other of God's children. Our people go off to carnival camps because they are afraid of getting their holiness tarnished, or because they are afraid to see the struggles of an unredeemed humanity displayed in certain aspects of the mas'. There is a refusal to have any sort of engagement or encounter with the 'undesirables' out of a blinkered attempt to preserve one's holiness. Jesus' ministry was one of engagement with the undesirables of society, the outcasts and the jamettised culture; with prostitutes, publicans, lepers and beggars. But if the church refuses to see then it lives in a false reality which segregates God's people into those who are good to keep and those good only to throw away. It is a false reality where sin and struggle with sinful institutions are non-existent. It is a deist approach that sees in God a means of merely transferring the burden of the world's problems and thus humanly avoiding them.

Following on the heels of celebrated masman Peter Minshall's presentation of 'Hallelujah' in 1995, calypsonian David Rudder produced an even more controversial recording of his hit song, 'High Mas', a pun on the words High Mass, the more solemn and ritualistic Roman Catholic / Anglican celebration of the Eucharist. His understanding was that Carnival was the people's offering of thanksgiving to God for the gift of festivity and merry-making. Moreso it was the Jamettised society offering, as suggested in the line, "See the ragamuffin congregate." Its music was couched in a version of Gregorian chant, so as to give the feel of a High Mass, against the background of a Soca beat, and complete with the people's response of, 'Amen', after each petition. The resulting combination and subsequent rendition is eclectic and full of the people's passion, that it would make for a thunderous chorus of praise if transferred into the church's liturgy, especially the Reformed, and thus give the liturgy a more Trinbagonian feel and nature. This particular song underscores Carnival's essential nature to the people's being and understanding of themselves and of society's make-up, and all of this unashamedly before God, who alone can heal, transform and renew. Of course it met with condemnatory opposition from the Puritan party as rubbish and rot, and goes to show the church's continuing failure to understand the society, preferring rather the Augustinian dichotomy, echoed by Von Allmen, of the City of God where people forego all earthly pleasures for the sake of pure Christian ideals, which he [Augustine] would think appropriate in his own mind, versus the City of Man, unredeemable and full of 'pagan' living, which is destined for doom. The calypso is cited here in its full version because it bears witness to God's incarnation among his people and of his engagement with them, remembering that the word and notion of 'incarnation' means the taking on of 'flesh', not only of physical flesh and blood but also of human nature. David Rudder captures the theology of Carnival poignantly when he sings:

> *"Our Father who has given us this art*
> *So that we can all feel a part*
> *Of this earthly (lesser) heaven…Amen*
> *Forgive us this day our daily weaknesses*
> *As we seek to cast our mortal burdens on this city…Amen*
> *Oh merciful Father, in this bacchanal season*
> *Where some men will lose their reason*
> *But most of us just want to wine and have a good time*
> *While we looking for a lime, Because we feeling fine, Lord…Amen*
> *And as we jump up and down in this crazy town*
> *Send us some music for some healing…Amen*
>
> *Our Father who has given us this art*
> *So that we can all feel as if we are a part*
> *Of your heaven…Amen*
> *Forgive us this day our daily weaknesses*
> *As we seek to cast our mortal burdens on this painful city…Amen*
> *And on this day when we come out to play and sway*
> *And do a little breakaway*
> *Some will say what they have to say*
> *But only you know the pain we're feeling…Amen*

As it was in the beginning of J'ouvert
So it shall be on Carnival Tuesday ending (good vibes)...Amen

Chorus:
Everybody hand raise
Everybody give praise
Everybody hand raise
And if you know what I mean...put up your finger
And if you know what I mean...put up your hand
And if you know what I mean...put up your finger
And if you know what I mean then scream
O, give Jah his praises, O, let Jah be praised
O, the Father in his mercy
Send a little music, to make the vibration raise
So Carnival Day, everybody come and celebrate
Everybody come and celebrate
See the ragamuffin congregate
Everybody come and celebrate
And everybody say, oo, a, a, oo, a, a, I love my country
oo, a, a, oo, a, a, I feeling irie (repeat)" (13)

Carnival involves another complex aspect of one's sense of being; that of breaking established taboos, crossing lines of demarkation, venturing into the forbidden, deviating from the norm and, choosing to become, not just simply to be. In the pre-emancipation celebrations when it was wholly the provenance of the plantocracy, there was the custom of portraying the roles of the slaves and a general parody of African culture and society. With the advent of African participation the tables were turned with the Blacks mimicking their White counterparts. Sexual boundaries were crossed in transvestism and flirtatious homosexual behaviour which are still a 'fun' part of the celebrations. Maureen Warner-Lewis remarks that since the Dame Lorraine and Baby doll characters were originally portrayed by men and as such considered anti-social shows an aspect of West-African secret society that allowed women to indulge periodically in sexual and verbal licence and for men to indulge in transvestite behaviour (14). On many occasions the breaking of established norms and practices are facilitated by the wearing of masks which hid the true identity of the perpetrator and therefore punishment cannot be apportioned appropriately. In any event, the general excuse that it is Carnival and anything goes! Here masks take on a spiritual dimension that they had in primitive cultures, of warding off spirits who would otherwise be offended by such taboo breaking, especially where their provenance might be encroached upon and keeping identities unknown and the perpetrators safe. Closely related to the notion of breaking taboos is the idea of deviations from the social norms. This, the Trinidad Carnival notes, is a major factor in the preponderance of women taking part in the festivities, as carnival allows them an opportunity, under the mask, to deviate from the regularly expected duties of marriage and family life, of being the ones who go to church to pray for the men [who can't be expected to go to church and still do what other menfolk expect of them]. *"Thus whilst the religious significance of Carnival is unimportant for the men it is highly significant for the women. It is their annual opportunity to do all that the Church and society condemns, and, further, it encourages them to participate with so much feeling and outward show of devotion in the yearly religious climax of Lent and Easter."* (15).

The wearing of the mask allows for the expression of the hypocritical duality of human nature. This is true hypocrisy at its best, true acting. The hidden aspects of human nature that would not normally be allowed or shown in regular social intercourse are freely transgressed. The true hypocrite is not the character portrayed or the act performed or experienced on Carnival day, but the person who re-enters regular society afterwards and shows disdain and contempt for what one has experienced under the mask, because by then, his / her identity would be revealed and there would be no covering to mask the shame. The Cartesian formula of Rene Descartes, 'Cogito ergo sum', 'I think, therefore, I am,' becomes in reality, 'Sum ergo cogito', 'I am, therefore I think', in this conflict between 'sum' and 'cogito' expressed in the mas'. In the desire to become and not just to be, at Carnival time, it is the person, because of who one is that one desires to become. The person is already possessed of innate desires and yearnings that are given expression under the mask. One can only conceive of what one is already possessed of and therefore is a subject with a self to acquire and not an object to be known. So that one can agree with Selwyn Cudjoe here when he says, *"This underground eruption of the culture represented a moment when the masses of people began to assume their original selves and asserted the integrity of their being. For women specifically, it meant the expression of female independence that was threatened by official society."* (16). It begs the question of a person's essence rather than just mere existence. The African thus saw an opportunity to project onto the visible stage of society one's true sense and essence of being. The person creates oneself from faithful awareness of one's heritage, environment and of all one's desires and urges and cultivation of one's inner potentialities which are then projected outwards.

Storytelling is as old as humanity itself, for before humans could learn to write, everything was passed down orally. Stories are thus the soul of a people, telling who they are and from whence they came and what they are like and how they think and act. They also entertain and like music and art give vent to all the passions and emotions of human existence. No small wonder that Trinidad and Tobago Carnival is a potent forum for and conveyor of the stories of the peoples of this land; not only in the incarnation of their struggles and representation of the social reality, but also in terms of telling a tale, dreaming a fantasy or weaving a plot that fires the imagination, tickles the senses and invigourates the spirit. The old mas' characters of J'Ouvert morning each tells a story either of political or social commentary, or of fancy, but filled with pun, parody, sarcasm and satire. So too do the bands of Carnival Tuesday with their 'pretty mas' each section adding a new dimension to the overall theme of the particular band and bringing to life a flight of fancy, thus enabling the masquerader to realise a desire of becoming. This is unchoreographed street theatre at its best. There is no script, no form of artificiality, just the freedom of being and expressing. And for all the Christian fundamentalist denunciations against the Harry Potter sagas as being replete with occult inferences and therefore having a bad influence on good Christian children, then maybe one would need to reassess all the familiar fairy tales of yore such as Cinderella, Snow White, Sleeping Beauty, Rapunzel and others for having witches, brews and spells in them, and which are simply expressions of the realm of fantasy which frees the human mind to imagine and conceive and devise.

In calypso also is this oral tradition taken to its peak. The calypsonian is first and foremost a storyteller who, using any theme or situation, can tell a tale of enormous proportions. They are also the prophets of the society, the voice of the underclass, who in their social and political commentaries rage against the present injustices and inspire in the people a passion for a new humanity. One wonders if today there is not too much concentration on vitriolic social and political commentary to the detriment of telling stories. Similarly too is the criticism against the preponderance of the overly sensual and the banal in what is classed as Soca music, which is not really what the originator, Ras Shorty I intended when he fused Soul music rhythms with Calypso in the early 1970's. Such is seen in the over emphasis on wining and gyrating, "Wuk da waistline, roll dat bumper;' or the trite, 'Show me your hand, han', han', han, wine, wine, wine, wine, wine,' 'Put your flag in de air and wave, wave, wave, wave, in de air, in de air, in de air.' One also hears the criticisms levelled against too much beads, bikinis and feathers and no real costuming, masking or story behind modern band portrayals, only explicit sexuality. And while Carnival does have roots in the ancient fertility cults of primitive civilisations, a people without stories are a people without a soul. What do you tell your children at night, if you do not have a story?

This leads into another dimension of the Carnival that can be overdone, but which, if kept within perspective and not abused, shows a basic aspect and need of living in a human body; and those are rites of sensuality, sexuality, fertility and prosperity. They are ancient and are seen generally as pagan. But human beings are sexual beings and sexuality is necessary for the fulfilment of natural urges and desires as well as the procreation of the species. Human sexual fertility has long been linked to the fertility and prosperity of the land and the economy. Although the former is no longer seen as divinely impinging upon the latter with its basic nature worship understanding of temple prostitutes and the like, it is nevertheless mirrored in the ability of the earth to produce and of humanity to obtain wealth. Sexual activity was a prominent part of ancient religion, where fertility cults abounded and were used as a means of initiation into the cult, or of attaining a level of divine communion with a particular deity. Barrenness or infertility in the Old Testament was seen as a curse for both parties. A man would not be able to raise an heir to his property and so lose his legacy to another. A woman would be scorned and despised. So Abraham and Sarah, Hannah, Elisabeth and others prayed for children. And the book of the Song of Songs is dedicated to the love of man and woman as sacred and sublime, regardless of its allegorical suppositions.

The church has been biased in favour of virginity as a preference of God, as when the Virgin Mary conceives the Messiah; she is preserved inviolate for all eternity, as sexual activity would somehow taint her holiness. Jesus Christ could never be perceived as having been married or having had children, but as celibate for the sake of the kingdom of God. And, therefore, Christians were encouraged to emulate same. This was the view posited by the likes of St. Augustine who in his writings came to abhor sex after years of wanton libido (19), and of St. Thomas Aquinas who generally saw all women as evil, having led the man astray in the Garden of Eden, and even sex in marriage was sinful though winked at for the sake of procreation because better could not be done, (17). Theirs was a stoic reading of St. Paul in the New Testament, as a man who despised all pleasure as being of the flesh and therefore evil, Galatians. 5:17, Ephesians 2:3. For a conservative evangelical reading of Matthew 22:30 borrowed from the commentary of Thomas Aquinas, above, where Jesus is questioned by the Pharisees about the nature of human relationships in the resurrection (which they disavowed), radio speaker Quentin J. Everest described believers in Christ as 'future space dwellers'. "Jesus, in speaking about the nature of the resurrection body, said that the resurrected believers will be like the angels of God in heaven, i.e. asexual, non-marrying and non-reproductive." (18) Who ever said that angels were asexual, non-marrying and non-reproductive? Is it because they are spirit that we assume thus? Are we forgetting the 'sons of God', the 'elohim', of Genesis 6, who married and copulated with the 'daughters of men' and created a mutant race? Could they then not be able to copulate with one another and reproduce their own species? Who are the seed of the devil, Genesis 3:15, and the sons of the evil one, Matthew 13:38? Is God then, asexual and non-reproductive, who created us in his image, male and female (and, as sexual beings, in all that the phrase connotes), and has revealed himself in both motherly and fatherly images in the Bible, and of himself has eternally generated/begotten the Son, the second person of the Trinity, as all noted heretofore? This classic position of the Church would seem to say that sex is too sinful for heaven, as with all [pseudo] gnostic approaches to matter and form or the earthly sphere of existence. Does the ultimate revelation of Jesus eclipse the prior one given to Isaiah, who in chapter 11:6-9 talks about the wolf and lamb dwelling together, the leopard with the kid, the calf, lion and fatling all led by a little child; of the cow and bear feeding together and a sucking child playing over the hole of the asp and the weaned child's hand over the adder's den? Is this the same God giving a progressive revelation or two different, seemingly contradictory ones? Where do children come from if there is no human reproduction? Ah! God will fashion them by his power since sex is too sinful for heaven. And why is Yahweh not the only god in human religious thought to have had a child with a human female, moreso a maiden? Could he not have been more original, since Christians claim to rely on a superior and truer revelation than all that ever was or will be?

This aforementioned view has been bolstered by the classical Puritan desire to abstain from all vanity and worldly lusts. In traditional Presbyterianism organ music was abhorred as sinful and worldly and not allowed in Churches. Churches, worship services and vestments were stripped of all decoration and semblance of profanity so as not to obscure their true spiritual nature. J. I. Packer in his book, 'Among God's Giants, The Puritan vision of the Christian Life notes this Puritan austerity, *"Finally, [John] Owen scouts the idea that ornate buildings and rituals have, or can have, anything to do with the 'beauty' that God seeks and finds in the worship of his faithful people...*

The idea that ritual pageantry in services and decoration of church buildings is of itself an enriching of worship thus appears as a ludicrous irreverence. 'What poor low thoughts have men of God and his ways, who think there lies an acceptable glory and beauty in a little paint and varnish.' "(19). An attestation to this 'little paint and varnish' can be found in 'Greyfriars' of Trinidad', where it is said of the first Presbyterian church in the island in 1836, that, *"The seats were of the most approved presbyterian pattern, unvarnished and straightbacked..."* (20) And again, of the Bevington pipe organ installed in 1877 by Rev. Alexander Falconer, it was said, *"There was some controversy about the use of musical instruments in public worship, and the organ appears not to have been used until 1893."* (21)

The Hindu Kama Sutra or Book of Pleasure, was written within the threefold view that humankind should practice the three stages of life, namely: 'Dharma' or the performance of religious and other duty so as to obtain 'Moksha' or liberation from reincarnation, 'Artha' or the obtaining of wealth and knowledge, and 'Kama' the practice of giving and receiving pleasure through the five physical senses. It is mainly concerned with the perfecting of the art of sexual lovemaking but also sees this as being on the path to 'moksha' since human lovemaking would be on a different level from the instinctive, seasonal mating of animals. We see here that any attempt to classify 'LOVE' into 'carnal' and 'spiritual' would be arbitrary and unwarranted for in this Hindu concept, 'spiritual' love has its natural roots in the physical and its incorporation into the language and cult of worship places it on par with the divine, and so the sensuous is wedded to the sacred. And there is no dichotomy between the sacred and secular or profane or carnal, as with Christian thought (22).

Dutch Reformed missiology professor, Pieter Holtrop remarks whether Reformed theology, *"...is able to take people seriously, people as they are, people already touched by grace."* In other words does Reformed theology take the doctrine of creation seriously...or must we admit that the Calvinist doctrine of grace and redemption does not have anything to do with historic reality, other than plucking people out of this' realm of darkness'? It causes Andre Karamaga to question the widespread opinion, even within the mainline churches in Africa itself, that the African cultural/religious inheritance, when seen in the light of the gospel, was only to show darkness. (23). It is the mindset of Victorian and Edwardian prudishness that has cast this annual fertility cult of Carnival in a negative light and calls for its total abhorrence. Perhaps this ancient link between human sexuality and terrestrial fertility needs to be recovered in the light of humankind's over domination of the earth and plunder of her resources, the threat of Global warming and a depletion of natural fuels, the warming of the seas and the creation of barren land. Celebrations of human sexuality and fertility such as Carnival should become forceful reminders of our commitment to the maintenance and continuing fertility and prosperity of the earth, not necessarily with a specific theme as with Brian Mac Farlane's 2008 Band of the Year winning portrayal of, 'Earth: Cries of Despair, Wings of Hope", which itself was magnificent.

Traditionally one would expect to hear in church on the Sunday before Carnival, or Dimanche Gras, a sermon condemning the paganism of Carnival. The Revised Common Lectionary to which all mainline churches now subscribe commends this day as a celebration of the culmination of the season after the Epiphany with the Transfiguration of Jesus. It is a logical conclusion seeing that the season begins with the Manifestation of Christ to the Gentiles [Wise Men] and goes through several of his manifestations or revelations of his glory through his ministry on earth climaxing with his revelation as the Son of God on the Mount of Transfiguration. This glory refers not so much to 'shekinah' or splendour and majesty, as to 'chabod', or the presence of God among his people. In his transfiguration before Peter, James and John, Jesus gives a preview of the glory he had before his incarnation. He is transfigured into a bright, shining image brighter than the sun. In this he also reveals humankind's true estate which they are destined to regain in him; the original image and likeness of God in which they were created but which has become tarnished by sin. This is the ultimate call to become all that God originally intended for humankind. In a similar vein Carnival is also a call to become a more just and equitable society by unmasking the realities behind the masks. There is a common link between the revelation of the 'chabod', glory or presence of God in Christ in the liturgical season leading to the climax of Carnival and the festival of Carnival itself in the God who struggles with his people, who knows, understands and identifies with their longings, hopes, desires and frustrations, a God who lived in such a situation in Palestine. It is seen in a God who changes water into wine and thereby has power to transform the ordinary into the glorious. It is a God who engages actively with his people, the undesirables of society, neither scorning nor rejecting anything he has made; who even had a terrorist, Simon the Zealot, for a disciple, for that is what Zealots were to the Romans in that time. And out of this engagement God is able to bring healing and transformation to the twisted and distorted lives of the Jamettised society, portrayed in the ole mas'.

The festival of Carnival is a time for the annual purgation of the people. It is a time when after a year of pent up frustrations relating to a neo-slavery work environment, the pressures of family life, traffic jams, political and social tensions and so many other stress causing factors, there can be release and rejuvenation. It is a demonstration of the catholicity of the peoples of this land, of all races, cultures, and religious persuasions, social and economic backgrounds merging into one massive, pulsating force of energy, where there is absolutely no segregation or discrimination of any kind. One is not even able to tell the difference between vagrant and upper class, as the mask covers all, especially the mask of oil, mud and paint of the J'Ouvert / Monday festivities. It is a time for rejoicing and singing praise, in the words of Psalm 150, where everything that breathes, yea exists is called to worship and celebrate the One who lives among them, witnesses and shares in their pain and suffering, who is crucified for them and takes into his pinned body on the Cross, the tormented shape of their daily anguish. Remember that masman Peter Minshall received heavy criticism from the church for his band, 'Hallelujah' in 1995, because it was felt to be blasphemous to 'drag' the praise of God into the realm of obscenity, paganism and devil worship.

Carnival reveals the creative aspect of humankind's nature with the remarkable structures of skill and beauty in individual portrayals. It is a time when the industry of the people comes alive.

Long, tireless hours are spent designing and fabricating costumes, tuning and preparing steelband arrangements for the competitions and then having to go to regular work the next morning after little or no sleep, only to re-enter the vicious but beloved cycle over and again each evening. Trinbagonians have thus been labelled a Carnival people who live seemingly only for the mere pleasure of the festival and have a love for fêting and partying or for the next Carnival in another Caribbean island, North America or England, without any real substance in their lives. This should not be. For to be a Carnival people in the truest sense of the term would mean to transfer all that energy at Carnival time into the regular work ethic during the rest of the year and seek to become—again called to become—an all-round productive people, excelling to even greater heights than have already been achieved.

There have been calls to return Carnival to its original celebration period at the time of the Emancipation celebrations. But it is believed that by so doing, it would revert to the provenance of only one ethnic group and confined societal struggle whereas as it is now, it is the heritage of all the peoples of the land regardless, a truly democratic institution and a sign of unity among those who make their home here. It would also forever link the festival to the evil of slavery and the sugar plantation from which it has struggled to be free in all connotations, though it is still called to portray the oppression and injustice of the prevailing system at large. And while making it a pre-Lenten festival would no doubt conjure up pre-Christian [pagan], Christian and European images to a certain extent, it has become so indelibly linked to the national sense of being at this time and endemic to the annual rhythm of life, that one could not transfer its celebration without injuring the national psyche and landscape.

NOTES

1. J. J. Von Allmen, Worship Its Theology and Practice, Lutterworth Press, London, 1965; part 1: Problems of Principle, chapter 3, The cult, the end and the future of the world, section c, The Christian cult as the pardon and the fulfilment of non-Christian cults, pg. 75.
2. ibid.
3. Book of Common Order of the Church of Scotland, Prayers for use at Holy Communion, pg. 191, St. Andrew Press, Edinburgh, 1994.
4. Trinidad Carnival, Paria Publishing Company, Port-of-Spain, © 1988, Carnival in Nineteenth Century Trinidad, pg. 7.
5. ibid pg. 13
6. Selwyn Cudjoe Beyond Boundaries: The Intellectual Tradition in Nineteenth Century Trinidad, ch. 5, Jamettization of the Culture 1838-1851, pg. 90: Calaloux Publications © 2003.
7. Mighty Sparrow (Slinger Francisco), Slave 1963, verse 4.
8. Popular Kalinda (Stickfighting) chant, public domain.
9. Op. cit. no. 5.
10. Op. cit. no. 3, Introduction, pp. xiv, xv.
11. ibid.
12. Op. cit. no. 6.
13. David Rudder, High Mas', 1998
14. Op. cit. no. 4, Conclusion, pg. 184.
15. Op. cit. no 4, The changing attitude of the coloured middle class towards Carnival, pp. 96, 97
16. Op. cit. no. 4, pg. 88.

17. St. Thomas Aquinas, Summa Theologiae 11-11, 153-154: Internet Medieval Sourcebook; Fordham University Center for Medieval Studies, New York
18. J. Frederick Coombs, Behold He Is Coming, (c) 2004, ch. 7, The Believer's Resurrection Body, pp. 57/8.
19. J. I. Packer, Among God's Giants; The Puritan vision of the Christian Life (c) 1991, Kingsway Publications; ch. 15, The Puritan Approach to Worship, section 2, pg. 332.
20. Greyfriars of Trinidad 1837-1987, published by the Kirk Session of Greyfriars' / St. Ann's Church of Scotland, 1987, ch. 1, The Beginning, pg. 12.
21. ibid. pg. 14.
22. The Kama Sutra of Vatsyayana, trans. Sir Richard Burton and F. F. Arbuthnot; ed. J. M. Gould; (c) Gould 1963, Panther Books.
23. Pieter Holtrop, Mission as Life -In-Community: A Biblical Reflection, published in Reformed World, theological journal of the World Alliance of Reformed Churches, Geneva Switzerland, Volume 42, No. 2 June 1992, pg. 35.

WATER; SOURCE OF LIFE: SOCIO-ECONOMIC, THEOLOGICAL AND INTER-RELIGIOUS PERSPECTIVES

This essay won the second prize in the 2006 Georges Lombard Essay Competition of the World Communion of Reformed Churches and was first published in the Reformed World Theological Journal, Volume 57 (1), March 2007 © WORLD Communion of Reformed Churches. Reprinted with permission

Water is a unique element on planet earth. It makes possible the existence of all living organisms more than any other element of life. Indeed, the very absence of this element on other planets of the solar system may well preclude the non-existence of life forms on any of them. It is observed that only the planet Mars lies within the narrow temperature band that allows water to exist in its three states of liquid, solid and gas, but only the Earth is blanketed by a living, water-built biosphere in which the life force seems to issue from the water's evaporation, precipitation, run-off, seepage, plant transpiration, animal respiration, melting, freezing and flowing. Earth as humanity knows it is the only "Water Planet" in this galaxy and therefore the only one capable of propagating various life forms (1).

The Dublin Principles for Water has declared that water is a finite and valuable economic resource (2), which, although self-recycling through the process of evaporation and condensation back into rainfall, is not increasing in quantity. In other words, it is argued that nearly every molecule of the water that exists today for human consumption was present at the time when the seas formed the earth. This is due mainly to the, *"Dynamic hydrological cycle that bathes and supports all life."* (3). Also, this hydrological cycle yields only a fixed quantity of water per time period, which cannot be humanly improved though it may be depleted by human waste and pollution. It is estimated that just three thousandths (3/1000) of the Earth's water is available for human consumption. The rest is either highly inaccessible, unfit to consume or just too expensive to obtain (4).

Water is a unique element. It can be absorb other elements such as heat and cold thereby making it a vast energy storage bank. Other substances can be dissolved in it as with sugar and salt or be suspended therein (i.e. existing side by side with the water without changing the essential nature of either) as in the case of milk, juices and other liquid or semi-solid products. Seeing, therefore, that Earth is essentially a 'water planet' with just over seventy percent of its landmass covered in this element, and all of its life forms having their origin therefrom, and the human body itself is composed of about the same seventy percent with water; it becomes evident that our own preservation is closely and inextricably linked with the availability of water for all, regarding basic human needs and, with the preservation of this very limited and finite resource from which all life originates. Water is, literally, the source of life on Earth and vital for its sustainability, even of human survival, dignity and development. Indeed, *"The earth is the Lord's, and the fulness thereof, the world and those who dwell therein; for he has founded it upon the seas and established it upon the rivers."* Psalm 24:1-2.

The demands on this finite resource are enormous. Industrial purposes, food and energy production, human consumption, sanitation, jobs and recreation stake their claim. And when these demands are translated into actual figures they become startling indeed. Water resources are under pressure from steadily increasing population growth, economic activity and intensifying competition from water users. At the heart of this there is also the voice for environmental needs among these other users in the ecosystem. Then too, there are growing concerns about climate change and variability such as the Greenhouse Effect and 'El Nino' phenomena, floods and drought (5). Yet the amount of usable water remains invariably unchanged.

Socio-Economic Perspectives

It has been recognised that about one in six of the world's human population is without access to potable water and at least one half without adequate sanitation (6). Many of these are located in the poorer segments of the developed and the developing world. In some of these segments, however, this inaccessibility is often confused with the inability to obtain a developed, perhaps even luxurious supply of water as via in-house taps and modern and/or elaborate bathing and sanitation systems as against a truck-borne or community taps/wells supply which may have an invariable supply. This still does not detract from the fact that a least 1.2 billion people worldwide are without recourse to an adequate water supply requisite for basic human consumption and sanitation needs, if any supply at all in most circumstances. The adult human body is seventy-percent water, and this figure is higher for children, so that one may be able to survive a traditional biblical period of forty days without food, but only a few days without water (7). It is therefore essential to the very dignity of the human person that each one has access to an amount of water necessary for personal survival and development, before the needs of the larger user groups.

This would invariably place water allocation firstly within the realm of economics and the political will (or lack thereof) to combat vested economic interests in industry and foreign investment. The Dublin Articles recognise that within this principle it is vital to recognise the basic right of all humans to access to water and sanitation at an affordable price. Water must be seen as having economic worth. The non-recognition of its full value has led to wasteful and environmentally damaging uses up to the present (8). There must needs be a cost for managing a nation's water resources in such a manner as to ensure the availability of this resource on a sustainable basis. But would it be proper to levy such an assessment on groups and communities already disadvantaged by the inaccessibility thereof, and who are also on the lowest levels of economic empowerment? An inherent danger here is that of the privatisation of water allocation and management supply and services. Where this action of a privatised supply of water services has occurred, there has been steadily soaring increases in rates, water shortages and disconnection without concern or compassion for those who may be unable to afford such services.

Applying such an economic instrument to support thus disadvantaged groups would affect behaviour towards conservation and efficient usage, provide incentives for demand management, ensure cost recovery and signal the consumers' willingness to pay for additional investments in water services. It is an important means of decision-making that impacts on social aspirations as well. In a water-scarce environment, would it be right to give water to industrial giants as against the poor simply because they can afford to pay? Water allocation may not be most efficient when valued in economic terms alone or acceptable when made only on political grounds. Here the value of water is measured against the economic charge for use and services. The value of water rightly assessed would place decisions on its management and allocation now within the realm of natural justice, fairplay and even equity to a lesser degree, bearing in mind increased scarcity of supply and a reduction in conflict among users (9).

No longer would it be the first, second and third fruits for the strong and powerful only, but as a kingdom principle God intended that the first fruits should go to him, rightly recognising water as a gift of God, essential to the created order, of which humanity is only a fraction. The second fruits as it were would have to involve a co-ordinated effort among all interests concerned. This means that all government agencies with an interest in water usage, such as health, local government, agriculture, public utilities, water management institutions, industry and other user groups should clarify the entitlements, responsibilities and roles in relation to stakeholders (10).

Water uses are interdependent and must be considered together. When, however, responsibility for drinking water rests with one agency, irrigation with another, environment with one else and industry with yet another, it no doubt leads to unco-ordinated water development and resource development management resulting in conflict, waste and unsustainable systems. Grassroots involvement should be paramount here because local solutions regarding water and sanitation would then be made by local people who are most affected. This endeavour would clean up much of the bureaucracy, redundancy and separatedness of human and other resources with regard to water management and, ensure a sustainable use of the resource. This effort serves to highlight as well, the interconnectedness of all of life which post-modern society has maliciously dissected into various compartments often at seeming conflict with one another; only in a vain attempt to attain to some measure of human control over the elemental and other forces of the created order which was never originally God-intended.

Lastly, the "gleanings of the field" should demand an attitude that incorporates even the poor and disadvantaged, Leviticus 19:9-10. God demands the 'Right Use' of his gifts so that his providential nature would be glorified when all creation is cared for, looked after and receives in celebration a just and fair distribution proportionate to one's needs without wasting, polluting, greed or selfish indulgence, Ezekiel 34; John 10:10.

Lack of basic resources vital to human existence and development and in many instances wilfully withheld on political grounds poses a serious threat to a person's power in society and position in decision-making circles. On the other hand, such an empowerment could be seen also as a threat to a government's power and position where absolute power is tyrannically maintained. Such possible threats are thus controlled and a government consolidates its hold on power. The General Council of the World Alliance of Reformed Churches in its 1989 open letter to the children and young people of the planet had this to say, *"Over and over again one refrain persisted: The rich get richer, while the poor get poorer. Surely the world should not be the way that it is. But if the world is to be changed…then the present global economic order will have to be altered drastically. Basic to all other injustices today…is economic injustice; and this means that churches are being called to recognise that the present world economic order and the systems and structures which maintain it are unjust at base. …They not only allow but they actually foster injustice in terms of the distribution of wealth and access to economic power. This means that people are bound to be kept in a condition of utter poverty while a few enjoy immense wealth. If the present economic order is maintained, this enormous discrepancy between rich and poor will prevail, and it will become still more conspicuous."* (11). Decision-making on water management and allocation must not be confined to vested interests of limited groups of users, geographical boundaries, sectoral institutions or national jurisdictions. It must involve full public consultation and decisions from the lowest levels of water users in planning and implementation. This would go a long way towards a rejection of the notion and experience of victimhood by the disadvantaged who desire to be on an equal footing with the rest of the world, at least where the equitable distribution of the earth's resources is concerned.

It may be that the powerful transnational economic trading blocs, economic superpower nations and even despotic regimes will keep setting objective standards that disempowered concerned groups and other such lobbyists cannot fight and who are to be mourned for protests so seemingly helpless. In any event, too, such protest actions appear to have only a hollow, passing effect in that there is a great uproar about a particular issue of a particular time-period, and without influencing the desired decision from the world power-houses, the protest dies or fades away quietly until another time and another issue. This can be seen with regard to the issue of the depletion of the Ozone layer, the refusal of the United States of America to sign the Kyoto Accord and the Jubilee 200 campaign to cancel the debts of poorer nations.

The Dublin Principles again bears witness to the need for gender equality with regard to water allocation and the concomitant empowerment that it brings to those so disadvantaged. It recognises that water management is male dominated because of a preponderance of males in the decision-making strata of government and its agencies and in industry and agriculture. It acknowledges, too, that different societies, especially more traditional ones, assign particular social, economic and cultural roles to men and women, and that there is need for synergy between gender equity and sustainable water management, where such gender equity would be improved by access of both men and women to water and water related services to meet their particular and essential needs (12). Women the world over have traditionally been revered as guardians of the living environment in their role as 'Mother'. They have been at the bedrock of sustainable development on the whole as homemakers, and through their involvement in agriculture. They thus play a central role in the provision, management and safeguarding of water.

Water, while not the source per se, can also be the means by which disease and death-carrying species of life are borne. Medical researcher David Bratt observes that water-borne diseases are 'dirty-water' diseases, caused primarily by water that has been contaminated by human, animal or chemical wastes. Worldwide the lack of sanitary waste disposal and of clean water for human consumption and hygiene is to blame for over twelve million deaths a year (13). He surmises, *"Water, like honesty or trust, when not contaminated with garbage, is healthy, clear and sparkling with life."* (14).

The fact that much of human activity with water and interference with many of the self-maintaining processes of nature, and with nature in general, has long been accepted as part of humankind's God-given right to take, have and hold dominion and subjugation of the Earth, Genesis 1:28. The construction of the Aswan High Dam in the River Nile has greatly affected the natural flooding of the plains with the river's silt and thus greatly reduced the agricultural capacity of the land to feed its people, resulting in widespread famine, malnutrition and disease. This is all due to the silt that would once fertilise the land now being deposited and trapped in the dam, and which also poses a problem to the infrastructural safety of the dam itself. More than a century earlier the transplanting of the Water Hyacinth from its unique home in the Orinoco River in Venezuela to other parts of the world because of its natural capacity as a water purifier has led to the plant now becoming an agricultural pest and a threat to many species of water life. The plant was removed from its place in a naturally controlled environment where seasonal flooding, insects, fish and others would feed and otherwise use the plant thus constricting its untamed spread that occurred when it was transplanted to other thus uncontrolled environments.

In 1825 the Erie Canal in the northern United States was opened with much fanfare celebrating the arrival of easier inland access through riverboats. Unseen however, was that with the opening of the Great Lakes to the Atlantic Ocean led to their invasion by the Sea Lamprey. This was a seafood delicacy in Europe from time immemorial, and unknown as such in North America. It soon became a ravaging parasite that greatly affected the fishing industry in the Great Lakes region for many years (15). These serve to highlight an idea of the Earth as a dead, empty thing to be conquered and subdued, (much the same way as women were regarded and treated in Western church and society), by the political and private economic giants that have continued the old imperial trends in a modern and brazen resurgence of neo-colonialist tendencies. Yet the apostle Paul reminds us that it was not only humankind that was redeemed by the Christ Event but all of creation which has been groaning in travail until the dawning of a new order, Romans 8:19-23.

Furthermore, Anne Hadfield, writing in Reformed World reminds us that this process of reconciliation to God is not a completed one either; but rather a continuing one that involves not just personal repentance but the twin-movements of stopping the destruction of creation and the restoration of creation, which would imply a christology of nature as well (16). This idea, as well as that of humankind as stewards of God's creation rather, is fully embodied in the church's eucharistic rite where not only thanks is invoked on behalf of the whole created order, but where this whole creation is together the sum total of the 'oikoumene'. In the words of Psalm 150 it is everything with breath that praises the Lord. The other psalms just previous to this last one also invoke the elemental forces of nature, with its flora and fauna in a universal thanksgiving. Indeed, "All creation rightly gives you thanks and praise; all life, all holiness comes from you" (17), and joins humanity and the entire cosmic order now in the ecstasy of the angelic 'Sanctus'. Therefore, it is the fulness of the benefits of the redemption of Jesus Christ that not only has been gained for the whole created order but also poured forth in eucharistic blessing through the intercession and elemental partaking of the priests and stewards of this creation, namely humankind; and more particularly those in direct communion with Christ, Romans 8:19ff; Revelation 22.

Theological Perspectives

There are two things essential to life: water and breath. Interestingly one of water's two component elements is that which is also responsible for sustaining 'everything that has breath', namely oxygen. These two elements of water and breath have formed the basis of a powerful biblical metaphor relating to the second and third persons of the Trinity, the spiritual life of humanity and the whole created order and also of life in communion with Jesus Christ.

In the beginning at the world's creation, it is the Spirit (ruach, breath) of God that hovers over the vast expanse of water, making it fertile to receive the life-giving word of God and bring all things into being. This 'word' of God itself is composed of water and breath as are all words and sounds that proceed from the mouth of any being. The two primordial elements of water and breath combine to incarnate thoughts into the spoken word. In the book of Job, chapter 37, verses 9 and 10, it is written that from God's chamber comes the whirlwind, and cold from the scattering winds (bringing water in their condensation) and by the breath of God ice is given, and the broad waters are frozen fast.

In anticipation of the New Creation in the Christ Event, this same Spirit is involved in the incarnation of the very 'Word' of God, the second person of the Trinity. He/She [the Spirit] was there in the inspiration of the prophets, the conception of Jesus and the pre-natal anointing of John the Baptiser, the laudatory acclamations of Mary, Zechariah and Simeon and Anna. It is the Spirit that is, "Ready to give birth to all the word will say." (18). This Word of God, incarnate as Jesus of Nazareth was called upon to heal a man blind from birth according to John' gospel, chapter 9. Jesus spits on the ground and with the wet clay anoints the man's eyes for healing. The spittle is composed of water and breath and coming from one who is God's incarnate Word and full of the Spirit. Thus the Spirit of God is again seen bringing life to birth when water and breath from the Holy One is cast upon dry, infertile earth.

Jesus uses the metaphor of water to refer to the Spirit of God indwelling those who respond to God through him. It was a potent symbol in a land that encompassed the extremes of cold and heat, aridity and fertility, desert and oasis. Water has been an all-important and many times scarce resource so that its intrinsic value was fully recognised and appreciated by the entire region for generations on end. More interestingly his referrals to the gift of living or life-giving water, recorded in John 4:10, 13; 7:38-39; (which themselves are seen as a fulfilling of the prophecies of Isaiah 55:1-2; Jeremiah 2:13; 17:13 and Zechariah 14:8 and the desire of Psalm 23:2); stand in stark contrast to the existence of the Dead Sea in which no life can be found or sustained. Indeed Jesus proclaimed blessings on those who 'hunger and thirst for righteousness', in Mathew 5:6, since this life-giving water of the fulness of life in God through the Spirit is given to those who live within the Reign of God and seek, invoke and exude his justice and mercy as priests of the new creation. The rivers of the Garden of Eden are life-giving. The water from the rock provided much needed relief in the crossing the barren wilderness into the Promised Land. Water, even if it destroyed Pharaoh and his host, did give a new life to the Israelites. The Syrian Captain, Namaan was cleansed of leprosy in the waters of the Jordan, as was likewise the world cleansed in the deluge of Noah's day. Indeed as Amos declares in chapter 5 verse 24, *"Let justice roll down like waters and righteousness like an ever-flowing stream."*

This justice and mercy of God in life-giving water is further contrasted with God's judgement and indignation against sin and a life contrary to his will, in drought. The absence of this life-giving resource symbolises the absence of his favour, his Spirit, his Word and his life, as clearly perceived in the story of Elijah who called a drought upon the land for three and one half years as God's judgement upon the idolatry of his people. However water itself may also be used as a sign of God's judgement on the land. It is common among Caribbean church-going folk to describe the ravages of hurricanes as the judgement of God upon a particular people. Recently with the double ravaging of the island of Grenada in two successive years by hurricanes Ivan and Emily respectively, the church has been forced to ask whether this can really be declared as the judgement of God when there are other islands with worse sins than that one.

In any event they, along with volcanoes, earthquakes and other such violent natural phenomena, may also be seen as a way of the Earth cleansing, purging and renewing herself; in much the same way a human being would have naturally automated means of self-cleansing and preservation. Or it could very well be the Earth reacting vehemently against the interference with and inhumanity of the human race against nature itself. The Earth takes a judgemental reaction to pollution, waste, wanton abuse, misuse and pillage of the Earth's resources and of the continued domination by the rich few of the poor, helpless masses.

But on the other hand is there a way that we can see the glory of God in the power of water to give life as well as to destroy? Scripture does testify to the Lord who, 'thunders upon many waters,' and who, 'sits enthroned upon the floods', Psalm 29:3,10. Also the very floods and mighty waves of the sea and the thunders worship God and declare his power in Psalm 93. The hymnwriter Robert Grant reminds us,

"O tell of his might, O sing of his grace,
Whose robe is the light, whose canopy space.
His chariots of wrath the deep thunderclouds form,
And dark is his path on the wings of the storm." (19).

These frightening effects of nature are often a time to complain and murmur before and against God; a time for frenzied intercession to be spared, yet scripture testifies to their giving praise to God's almightiness in their potency, as also Job 36:27–37:24 concurs.

This multi-faceted imagery of water, its natural 'fluidity' to being adapted to various uses, its all pervading character throughout many states of being has led to its adoption in scripture by Jesus, John the Baptiser and others as a symbol of cleansing, renewal, promise and hope. And this is chiefly demonstrated and effected in the sacrament of baptism. Again Jesus makes the reference to water's intrinsic relationship to life and breath, (ruach—Spirit) in his notion that to be born again would be through the one baptism of these two intertwining principles, water and the Spirit. Indeed for the purposes of Christian theology, water may be the source of life, but water without the Spirit gives no real life at all. It is, thus, with a sense of grave concern that this writer pens one's deep disquiet over Reformed Ministers of Word and Sacrament who baptise without any thanksgiving over or epiclesis of the Spirit upon the baptismal waters, especially of a falsely perceived notion that it closely resembles practices of the pre-Reformation Roman church. In the creation narrative it is the life-giving Spirit who breathes upon the watery chaos and brings it into order. So that from the time of Jesus, life-giving water and the gift of the Holy Spirit must always be seen in the closest relationship possible since they are inseparable. But the Spirit must be invoked, called to breathe upon, and never taken for granted. Otherwise we run the risk of 'forsaking the fountain of living water', Jeremiah 7:13, and performing a mere ritual that is not an effective means of grace or potent to apply the thing signified to the recipient, though all the faith in the universe be present. The Reformed tradition has always evangelically held that sacraments and indeed the entire salvific economy of God and the church is effected primarily by the sovereign and graceful action of God perceived and obtained through faith, but that faith is never the centre of activity or point of departure. The same malpractice of the failure to have an epiclesis of the Holy Spirit is also true of many a Reformed celebration of the Eucharist.

Water may be further used as a metaphor of the Resurrection in the Caribbean. With the advent of Christianity and missionary activity in the colonial era the Caribbean church inevitably acquired all the trappings and imagery of a European brand of the faith. Within this were hymns and ideas relating to the changing of seasons of a temperate climate and especially of the significance of Spring as a time of new birth, fertility and resurrection in relation to the seemingly dead earth, delayed activity and suspended animation of the effects of Winter upon the land. This is totally out of harmony with the weather patterns of the Caribbean where only two seasons abound, namely Dry and Wet. Yet there is a similar deathlike quality over the land in the intense heat and dryness of the Dry season. Rain hardly falls, there is the threat of drought, water reserves are used up and water is rationed along with penalties for failure to observe such water rationing as with wetting of lawns and use of hoses. The land is parched and on many a mountainside and plain there are vicious bush fires, [hu]manmade or naturally caused. The grass dries up and the land is bare and hard. No planting takes place then. But then the Poui tree sends forth her blossoms in March / April and the people breathe a sigh of relief because the Poui signals the coming of the April showers with their promise of renewal, slightly cooler temperatures, especially at night and fertility.

The dryness of the land is intimately linked with the timing of the season of Lent and the Crucifixion and is a ready symbol of repentance, of yearning and thirst for living water, of death, loss, suffering and sacrifice. The advent of the April showers potently point to Christ who by his rising again becomes our Returning Rain and who comes to renew creation in all its colour and splendour. This Returning Rain also comes with victory to those who have known loss and destruction, whose lives are parched and dry from not having any more tears to cry or have grown hard and callous from pain and suffering. The Returning Rain comes to bring freshness and colour to those bound in the staleness of routine or lack of imagination.

Inter-religious Perspectives

Water, as a religious image is common to all religions, no doubt because of its recognition as essential to life and living. It is to be found in prayers, scripture texts, teachings and rituals. Whereas in Christianity water is only now being appreciated as a gift of God, it formerly being just another tract of subjugated creation, other religions have tended to see water as the sacred milieu in which we live. This is due to a pantheistic approach to creation which views the created order as divided aspects of the divine whole, each intrinsically divine in its own right and worthy of praise, awe, respect and therefore, right use. Christianity has tended formerly to regard only that water consecrated for spiritual use as in baptism or as holy water for cleansing, blessing and purification as sacred. Yet more traditional religions because of the people's closeness with the land and the elements of nature have preferred to give a more sacred character to water on the whole and to see it as an interconnected part of all life. It does not follow that all believers of such religions always observe the tenets of their respective faiths especially in regard to the right use nature. Throughout humanity there is ever the tendency to evil and destruction.

In Hinduism and in the Orisha religion (transplanted in the Caribbean from India and West Africa), rivers, streams, and oceans contain the vital mother spirit. From the churning of the seas the Hindu Mother Lakshmi, the feminine aspect of Vishnu, was generated. She is the mother of all, living and the goddess of wealth and prosperity. For the Orisha the water spirit is represented by the Kwéyol name, 'Mama Glo', from the French, 'Maman de L'Eau', mother of the water. This bears an interesting connotation to the biblical connection between water and the Spirit seeing that in Hebrew the generic word for Spirit is feminine in gender. But Mama Glo can be beneficent if her gift is used rightly or vengeful if abused. Water in Hinduism is worshipped as the source of all life. Originally revered at the mighty Ganges River as Ganga Dhaara in India, post-colonial Caribbean diaspora Hindus, who were believed to have lost their caste and by extension all ancestral and other connections with Mother India in crossing the seas, have reestablished that bond in this ritual of Ganga Dhaara. It purports that since all waters merge into one in the oceans then all water whether of river or sea and separated by landmasses are essentially one through this oceanic connection. So that the Ganges can be revered in the diaspora in this way. But for this writer, this ideology does not augur well for re-establishing the local validity of the land, lost through western imperialism, in itself, since it here has to get validity from a supposed connection with a foreign entity, seeing it once had a local identity and validity of its own.

For Africans transplanted to the West from their native continent by the demonic system of slavery and its concomitant racism, the crossing of the sea also signifies a cutting off of ancestral ties and the establishing of a new way of being though still intrinsically African, on new soil. For many it is the salt in the seawater that cuts, kills and even hinders. Added to water, salt takes away its potability and is effective also against spirits of evil. As the biblical prophet Elisha used salt to restore this potability to the Jordan, 2 Kings 2:21, so too salt added to water has traditionally been used in Christianity to convey blessing and warding off from evil in holy water. And in popular belief it is acknowledged that crossing the sea by any means of transport or even a sea bath is potent to cleanse from 'obeah', or witchcraft. For Orisha religion salt, in food or water, is never offered to the gods because it cuts off all spirit contact whether for good or for ill, (20).

The crossing, though, of a river, especially in a dream, often signifies death of some sort, physical or spiritual. There is also an interesting connection here with the biblical concept of crossing the Jordan into the Promised Land, used by Christianity as an image of passing over from death to eternity. And there is also the connection with baptism especially believer's immersion baptism, which is the defining rite of the large Afro-based indigenous Christian expression in the Caribbean, the Spiritual Baptist Shouter Faith. Here baptism refers to the uniting of the believer into the death, burial and resurrection of Jesus, Romans 6:3-11.

Conclusion

Water is a sacred gift from God to humankind, indeed to all life on the earth. As the guardians, stewards, priests of God's creation and acting thusly on behalf of the rest of the created order there is need to ensure that all life has access to the water it needs to preserve one's intrinsic dignity of being and the continuation in time to come of one's species. This requires a recognition of all life as being interconnected and that humanity are not dominators or the sole proprietors of God's sacred gift.; but that all life that depends on water in some form has a right to access it without fear or favour. As a gift it must be held in a similarly sacred trust and used rightly and managed properly, without wasting, polluting or destroying this already limited, overburdened and finite yet absolutely essential resource for life. Humanity, spearheaded by the church must continue to work and pray to ensure the justice, peace and integrity of God's creation, that there may be a just and equal sharing of all Mother Earth's resources for all her creatures and that *"The Earth will be filled with the knowledge of the glory of the Lord as the waters cover the sea."* Habakkuk 2:14.

NOTES

1. The Cousteau Almanac—An Inventory of life on our Water Planet: Water Facts pg. 116: Jacques-Yves Cousteau and staff of the Cousteau Society; Doubleday and Co. Inc. New York, 1981.
2. The Dublin Principles for Water—Statement on Water and Sustainable Development; International Conference on Water and the Environment, Dublin, Ireland, January 1992.
3. Op. Cit. no. 1, pg. 117.
4. Ibid. Eating, Drinking and Breathing, pg. 616.
5. Dublin Principles for Water as reflected in a Comparative Assessment of Institutional and Legal Arrangements for Integrated Water Resources Management: Miguel Solanes, Fernando Gonzales-Villareal, June 1999.
6. Ibid.
7. Article—The Source of Life: David E. Bratt M.D., published in the Trinidad Guardian Newspaper, 28/3/2006
8. Op. Cit. no. 5.
9. Ibid.
10. Ibid.
11. Justice, Peace and the Integrity of Creation: Report to the General Council—An Open Letter to the Children and Young People of the Planet; pg. 133 Reformed World, Section 111; volume 40, number 7, September 1989; published by the World Alliance of Reformed Churches, Geneva, Switzerland.
12. Op. Cit. No. 5.
13. Op. Cit. No. 7.
14. Ibid.
15. Op. Cit. No. 1, pg. 180ff: Unlearned Lessons—Unintended Effects.

16. Gospel and Cultures—A Perspective Form the Pacific; Anne Hadfield pp. 31/2: Reformed World; volume 46, number 1, March 1996; published by the World Alliance of Reformed Churches, Geneva, Switzerland.
17. Eucharistic Prayer B; Book of Common Prayer, Anglican Church in the Province of the West Indies, 1995.
18. Hymn, Enemy of Apathy; John Bell and Graham Maule: Wild Goose Resource Group, Iona Community: published in Iona Abbey Worship Book; Iona Community 2002.
19. Hymn, O Worship the King, all-glorious above; Robert Grant 1779-1838; published in The Church Hymnary, third edition, Oxford University Press.
20. Guinea's Other Suns—The African Dynamic in Trinidad Culture; Maureen Warner-Lewis: The Majority Press, Dover, Massachusetts, USA, 1991.
21. All Bible quotations are taken from the New Oxford Annotated Bible, Revised Standard Version, Oxford University Press Inc., 1962, 1973.

ALEXANDER KENNEDY MEMORIAL LECTURE

Delivered by The Reverend Clifford R. L. Rawlins, Dip R S (Cantab.) Lic. Theol, At Holy Trinity Cathedral Church To mark the 175th Anniversary of the Arrival of The Rev'd. Alexander Kennedy, Pioneer Presbyterian Missionary to Trinidad and Founder of Greyfriars' Church, Port-of-Spain. Sunday 13th February 2011 at 4.00 p.m.

Whenever a religion enters new territory it inevitably comes with extra baggage. It would have attained a certain level of experience, evolution and acculturation in its previous setting, and would naturally carry these over into the new place, because that would be its character thus far. It would be romantic for it to enter each new phase of existence as purely and unadulteratedly as it first began, and thus give such new experience an unbiased opportunity to grow, develop, engage and encounter and assume an independent acculturation in each setting and a unique sense of being while maintaining, as would be the case with the Christian church, the common thread of doctrinal and ecclesial unity. But the culture which the church cannot simply take off like a garment is its European and Western culture formed previously from Jewish and Hellenistic Greek traditions and thought processes; which themselves were not untainted by other surrounding traditions and philosophies. The church cannot just strip off this historically contingent clothing and slip into some other new cultural garb, because there is no such thing as a Christianity existing a priori culture and history, or being culturally free.

Likewise, the past ought not to be viewed with modern eyes, supposedly more enlightened by developed human wisdom, knowledge and understanding, because those who lived at that time and espoused its world view, did not and could not have had the present understanding and enlightenment by which to judge and modify their actions. They were children of their day. If, however, past evils and negative outlook continue in the present despite the modern development then that is what must be corrected. We cannot judge and condemn past actions because they do not fit in to today's trend of thinking, which is what we have been doing with this subject of colonisation. What should be done is to learn rather from the past and hopefully not repeat its mistakes and thus improve and build on its foundations, or rebuild them if need be.

By the 1830's the Scots inhabitants of Trinidad were the most numerous among the British colonists and had often lamented that there was no Presbyterian presence on the island to cater to their religious needs and inclinations. A Trinidad Presbyterian Association was formed and a memorial was sent to the Governor, Sir George Fitzgerald Hill, in October 1833 asking that Presbyterian churches and clergy be provided for Trinidad from the Established Church of Scotland as has been the case in Guyana and Grenada. Indeed the minister of St. Andrew's, Georgetown, Guyana, Rev'd. Archibald Browne, who himself had also ministered in Grenada, paid a visit to Trinidad in that same year to assess the situation here. The matter was referred to the Colonial Office in London which claimed that it did not have sufficient funds to support a church here, for as with Guyana and Grenada, a minister of the established church would have to be appointed and supported by the state. As if by utter Presbyterian providential predetermination the United Secession Church in Scotland resolved in Synod of 1831 to encourage foreign mission work, "...to some part of the heathen world" (1), but deferred further action until 1834 because slavery was considered an impediment to missionary work among negroes in the West Indies (2).

There was no doubt to the implications of such a statement as by this time the British Protestant ethic had taken up the inevitable prophetic call of the gospel to recognise the intrinsic dignity of all God's human creation and was calling for slavery's abolition. Then the church could no longer adhere to the commands of the state to preach only the moral duties of slaves to masters, or an opiate gospel in which, "...the promises of God lead the slave to consider his temporal afflictions as momentary and transient, and not worthy of being compared with that eternal weight of glory which God has in store for all that love and fear him." (3) or again one which as noted heretofore was not willing to grant full church membership as that would confer equal status in the kingdom of God and the world order for persons considered as sub-human species. So that by the time Alexander Kennedy arrived he did not have to face those impediments and prohibitions of the state. This United Secession Church had seceded from the established one over the issue of patronage or the right of the congregation over and against the state's patron, to call a minister of their own. The idea of foreign missions was taken up by Greyfriars' Church in Glasgow in 1834 and in 1835 decided to send a missionary to Trinidad after having initiated missionary activity on the isle of Oban in the British Isles.

Alexander Kennedy, originally from Cumnock, Ayrshire, was ordained in Greyfriars' Church, Glasgow on 30th September 1835 for work in Trinidad and arrived here on 25th January 1836. Rev. Kennedy was not totally alone in this new land. His former roommate at Glasgow University, Robert T. McCowan was a medical doctor stationed with the 74th Regiment at San Fernando. Robert's father David McCowan had migrated to Trinidad in 1800 to seek his fortune as a mason, architect and importer. The McCowan family in Scotland were coalminers bound in a longstanding form of indentured labour to the coalmine that often involved entire families. The Cumnock mines were bound to the Earl of Dumfries. An Act of Parliament in 1799 gave them unconditional emancipation and David took advantage of the new economic order that was afforded by the territorial expansion of the British Empire. He married a Sarah Thomas Packwood in 1808 and had a son Robert in Trinidad whom he sent to be educated in his native land, as has been the European custom. It would appear that on the rejection by the Colonial Office sponsorship of a Presbyterian ministry by the established church, Robert McCowan contacted his old friend, and all things being providentially equal, was responsible for Alexander Kennedy and the United Secession Church's coming to Trinidad (4).

Kennedy immediately set about the task of gathering a congregation and building a church. He assesses the situation immediately, noting, "Trinidad is a land in almost pagan darkness and Port-of-Spain is truly a missionary field but of a very peculiar kind. Here you may daily witness in bold relief the two extremes of human society—rudeness and refinement. With a few honourable exceptions, the black and coloured population are notoriously ignorant and unblushingly immoral. On the other hand, the more wealthy and influential members of the community, principally from Europe and America, are devotees of etiquette and fashion. Their minds are generally well-informed and their tastes delicate even to fastidiousness in all things that come under the indefinite laws of honour and gentility; but of their morality I cannot speak so freely; here is exhibited the greatest amount of moral destitution and delinquency. The situation of a faithful Minister here will prove one of peculiar delicacy and difficulty—one in which talent and faithfulness will be severely taxed and wisdom greatly needed." (5).

In 1839 Kennedy organised the Greyfriars' Missionary Society immediately began to reach out to the newly emancipated citizens by establishing preaching points at Belmont (Freetown Valley) where a church was subsequently built and is at present defunct, the site being used as the Belmont Police Station, East Dry River in the Quarry Street area, Tucker Valley, St. James Road and at Arouca and San Fernando. In Belmont, Kennedy first hired for a mission station the house of an African Black Art Doctor (6). And while his tradition was opposed to Roman Catholicism he nevertheless used the house of a Roman Catholic widow for his mission station in the Quarry Street area and spoke of her, "...with tender Christian solicitude trusting she was a child of God." (7). Clearly, he did not see Roman Catholicism in the harshly puritannical terms of being a false church and the pope as the antichrist as decreed then by the Westminster Confession of Faith, the Church of Scotland's subordinate doctrinal standard. His method of engagement with the African inhabitants was not of the regular missionary ilk. Kennedy was prepared to relate with this new people he encountered on an equal footing to his own people and was determined to make his church a place where they would experience such equality in worship, ministry and seating arrangement, unlike at Trinity Cathedral where they would have to walk with their own chairs and be afforded seating at the back, or in the forecourt. At Greyfriars it was an African who carried in the Bible to the pulpit before the minister's entry in the simple Presbyterian processional, and at his mission stations he used such young men to conduct prayers in the vernacular (this could be either the French patois, or the various languages of the predominant Rada community of Belmont -Ewe, Fon, Kikongo- or Yoruba etc. (8), and to address a few words to the congregation (9). In this way Kennedy foresaw the importance of an indigenous church and ministry, ministering to and among one's own people in one's own peculiar way as the most effective means for conveying the gospel in any given local setting. His method was, in effect, one of planting, equipping and enabling a local church to be the church where it was. It was not in the common style of a European-foisted gospel by a more illumined race that was messianically charged with conveying the gospel to persons in 'heathen darkness', and even where a native ministry was encouraged and equipped, would be kept as mere assistants to the White expatriate missionary from the church in charge of the local missions. Kennedy was a man ahead of his time and therefore could not have survived in an environment that was unprepared and unready for such a radical reintroduction of the apostolic model of Christian evangelisation.

By the time he arrived however, it was too late to engage in the prophetic polemics against the perpetuation of slavery, as the slave trade was abolished in 1807 and slavery itself in 1834. But Kennedy encountered an enigma of a strange kind. While slavery was virtually abolished, the ex-slaves could not leave the plantation for a further six years, initially. They were 'tied' to their masters by an Apprenticeship System. This was proposed under the guise of wanting them to learn a viable trade for their economic ingrafting into the newly emerging society and to prepare them, in a way, for their freedom. Harold Sitahal notes, "...The theological misconceptions of Wilberforce were greatly responsible for this gross miscarriage of justice...In the case of the Negro slaves the soil must be prepared for the reception of this 'plant of celestial growth'. So, in order to grant freedom to them 'a previous course of discipline is necessary.' Wilberforce, therefore set the course for emancipation, apprenticeship and missionary programmes for the rest of the 19th century based on preparing the native soil for freedom, 'that plant of celestial growth'. In Wilberforce's words the Negroes 'must be trained and educated for this most perfect state of manly maturity.' " (10). It would be this sentiment that would come to haunt the newly freed peoples as they sought to integrate into parts of the civil order once held as 'sancto sanctorum' by the Europeans, because they would never be ready enough and always condemned to level of assistantships, never fully in charge, and which would linger on in the post-independence neo-colonialist Caribbean mindset.

Writing of Rev'd J. C. MacDonald in 1917, Hamid quotes one of his letters of 1917, "...the senior missionary in San Fernando believes that to put an East Indian in Susamachar [the Presbyterian church of the Canadian Mission in San Fernando, and premier Presbyterian pulpit in that denomination] would be unfortunate, but facts are facts and we must face them. And then, every other Church in this town has a white minister." (11). The Susamachar congregation had called one of its native ministers, Rev'd. Charles D. Lalla as its minister but this was papistically overturned by MacDonald.

The situation was not limited to the Presbyterian experience. Selwyn Cudjoe writes of the Rev'd. Canon Philip Douglin who had been an Anglican missionary to West Africa and who in 1887 was appointed as Rector of St. Clement's Church in Naparima, whose appointment was protested by George Townsend Fenwick, member for Naparima and planting attorney for the Colonial Sugar Company, to the effect that he and his white colleagues could not worship under the pastoral care of a black man (12).

But the Apprenticeship system would also serve to cushion the plantocracy from the drastic immediate effects of abolition by allowing a gradual move off the plantation by the ex-slaves, as the colonial government sought ways and means of compensating them for economic losses and readjustments incurred. There would be no talk however of any kind of compensation for the disenfranchised ex-slaves. The focus was on the well-being of the planter at the expense of creating a bastardised, peasant society and culture which although free, for all intents and purposes, would nevertheless be subjected to the lower rungs of the feudal or at least by then, the civil order that put the European first and sought to maintain that ascendancy at any and all costs. Because naturally the European was of a superior race, religion and culture. But Kennedy, like his friend Robert McCowan's family, had known and experienced virtual slavery in the tied coalmines of Cumnock, his family being tenants on the farm of Dalricket Mill. He had firsthand experience of such inhumane treatment of other human beings in a feudal order that was already becoming archaic in view of American independence 1776, the French Revolution of 1789, the overthrowing of Spanish domination in South and Central America and, rumblings at home for Scottish independence from the union with England of 1707. He also had his church's stance on slavery being an impediment to missionary activity. He was also from a very strong 'Covenanting' tradition in Scotland which challenged the state for decades following the Scottish Reformation of 1560 for the establishment of presbyterial church government against episcopacy and which eventually won with the signing of the 'National Covenant' in 1638 which has safeguarded the character and ethos of Scotland's official Presbyterian religion. So Kennedy knew what it was to challenge and win against the might of secular kingdom and empire at the height of its imperial glory and expansion and to not have the state ever challenge such "martyr-able" determination of the church.

Armed with these determining factors he therefore became influential in the formation of the Anti-Slavery Society which met in Greyfriars' Church as its base and with widespread collaboration across the Caribbean succeeded in getting the British government to reduce the Apprenticeship System by two years to four instead of the original six. More than any other missionary of the time Kennedy appropriated the art of apostolic engagement/encounter even though he might be chided for not being fully appreciative of the "others in their otherness", as a European nonetheless. He became a trusted and beloved friend of the African community, as

Hugh Cameron acknowledges, "Came a time when the apprentices decided to revolt—but consulted Kennedy. For 24 hours, said he, he was virtually Governor of the Island: for only he could dissuade them: which he did—to the salvation of both sides—by persuading them that if they revolted their eventual condition would be worse than before." (13). On Wednesday 1st August 1838, Emancipation Day, Kennedy preached to the newly freed masses and others from Exodus 13:3, "Remember this day, in which you came out from Egypt, out of the house of bondage." Here Kennedy tapped into the very soul of the Afro-Caribbean slave experience. The former 'opiate gospel' manipulated by imperialism had manifested an inherent grace that no amount of human distortion could deny or erase. The gospel by itself is the very, '…power of God to salvation to everyone who has faith…" Rom. 1:16. All human accretions stand powerless to this inherent grace because it is the very all-conquering word of God himself. Its message would thus give meaning and credence to the African slave's appropriation of the 'opiate gospel' in terms of, "the hope that does not disappoint," Rom. 5:1-5, because "God will make a way somehow, where there seems to be no way". Alexander Kennedy captured the heart of Black preaching and his identification and analysis of Black hopes and aspirations in the text of his Emancipation Day sermon was accurate, as Bishop Frederick Talbot of the African Methodist Episcopal (AME) Church deduces, "It is through preaching that Black people are given hope as they struggle against oppression in society; as they gather to hear that God is incarnational and is present in their struggles; that God loves them, and shares in their common life and pain. It is through preaching that Black people are taught to rehabilitate their values 'for themselves', and to reroot themselves within a history, within a geography, within a culture. It is through Black preaching that Black people have their dignity reinforced: are reminded that their personhood is authentic; that they are persons of present and ultimate worth; that they have a responsibility one to another in the conception of 'collective self'; …It is through Black preaching that the memories and hopes of the community are kindled and that God is glorified as the God who redeems, enables, liberates and sanctifies. It is through Black preaching that Black people hear with 'appropriate' rhythm and passion that 'God will make a way somehow'—'a way out of no way.' It is through Black preaching that the lofty metaphors of God and Jesus Christ are repeated as 'realised eschatology.' " (14).

And yet it was not so much solely identifying with the Anti-Slavery cause that constrained Kennedy to engage in such prophetic utterances; it was the very nature of the prophet with which he was anointed. Such prophetic preaching could not be expected to adhere to the status quo and divorce religion from the life of the world, as if to spiritualise salvation as relevant only to the soul and not the body; the whole 'pie in the sky' idea. But this was the expectation of the ruling class of the day and of every day and generation which seeks to maintain control and hegemony at any and all costs. This was evidenced by the condemnation of Kennedy's Emancipation Day sermon in the Port-of-Spain Gazette, which further preposterously attempted to demarcate the boundaries of a minister's calling. "To incite his hearers to the practice of the different duties of morality and religion—refraining from controversy on those doubtful or disputed points which will ever divide mankind, and above all, seizing no occasion or pretext to exhibit that sort of equivocal benevolence which consists in telling one part of the community that they owe no obligation, and consequently no gratitude, to the other part; to incite his hearers, we repeat, to the practice of the different duties of morality and religion, the great object of all creeds, and to refrain from observations tending to weaken them, is the only duty of a preacher, which will meet with general approval in the nineteenth century. We dismiss the subject, not without hope that we should be compelled to return to it again."(15). A good preacher will not 'rock the boat' or 'trouble the waters', but 'knowing where his bread is buttered', will ever seek to soothe his hearers with the finer, softer points of Christian duty even if society rots all around him. His business is with the sphere of the church, society's business is that of those who are not called to religion. Somehow the realities of the latter did not impinge on the former whose primary concern was that of the afterlife!

Colonial religion seeks to divide the world into two spheres, the sacred and what is called the 'secular', a most misunderstood and misused word but which had become entrenched in use in this way that it is difficult to reverse it. This is the Church speaking with the voice of Empire which divides in order to maintain control and which gives 'secular' powers, authority over religion It was not the experience of Kennedy's Scotland which held two separate but equal realms of Church and State over which Christ exercises supreme overlordship. Indeed this is the biblical model of the cosmic Christ post-resurrection as found throughout the New Testament and which builds on the Jewish concept of a theocracy.

Imperialism was likened to the tyranny of Egypt that was virtually wiped off the face of the earth by the power of a God who moves on the stage of human history and assuredly acts on behalf of powerless and oppressed people who cry to him for deliverance; whom the slaves were. This prophetic voice was a recapitulation of God's mighty acts in delivering the Israelites from Egyptian bondage; an experience the ex-slaves appropriated most intimately, and the heart of Black worship is found in this sense of hope where God is the all-powerful, unconquerable, sure and certain Liberator and Deliverer of the oppressed. But the African ex-slave was likened to more than that. In comparing them with the children of Israel, the Old Testament covenant people of God, Kennedy was in fact saying that they were children of God; a royal, chosen, covenant people with whom God has a special relationship and conveys special covenant blessings, and therefore a people conferred with anointed human dignity and self-worth. He was saying that they had a definite place, turning point and recreation in history when they would begin a new search for selfhood and self-determination to which they could always look back and draw reference from, even as the Israelites could always point to the Exodus for their definite, historical creation as God's people. It was a definite point in history in a definite but new geographical setting. It would be a 'rerooting' of an uprooted people, charting a new course of history in a new world and economic order.

Rev'd. Kennedy also commended to these oppressed people a prophetic experience of God as Liberator and Champion of the Poor;

which view of God would fuel and shape their hopes and desires in the Labour movement and subsequent riots and liberation preaching of Tubal Uriah Buzz Butler in 1937, the Independence movement, Black Power Revolution of 1970, and all subsequent attempts for selfhood and equality by any trampled people. Kennedy's sermon, unsurprisingly, met with uncanny denunciation in the press (the Trinidad Standard and the Port-of-Spain Gazette) to the effect that "…he had spoken in a manner that was calculated to engender feelings of hostility between the recently freed slaves and their future employers." (16). He admitted that he did "handle slavery without gloves" (17), but was grossly misrepresented, and his protest as well as the entire text of the sermon was published for sale along with the Report of the First Public Meeting of the Trinidad Auxiliary Anti-Slavery Society of which he was president. Among the protests to the misrepresentation of the sermon by the press, is this one, "The report of his sermon in the Standard is a most gross misrepresentation and contains ideas to which he did not give utterance. His language also is glaringly perverted and mis-applied—the whole tenor of his discourse having been calculated to promote adherence to the laws of God and Man and to advance the religious, moral and intellectual condition of those whom he addressed." (18). By challenging the feudal and civil order of the day Kennedy engendered hostility among his fellow Scots colonists because his was not 'ministerial-like behaviour'. The Greyfriars' Historical Sketch booklet notes, "Kennedy's defence was, 'Why should I forfeit my privileges as a citizen simply because I am a minister of religion?' During his furlough in Scotland in 1841, he[9] scathingly criticised in a sermon the attitudes of the Scots colonists, and on his return to Trinidad found that he had lost much of his congregation. Because, however, he championed the cause of the underprivileged Blacks, they always filled his church to overflowing." (19). Perhaps Kennedy was not so sure that the freed ex-slaves should continue to work for their White masters in some form or other. He would have had in mind the experience of the emancipated coalminers in his native Cumnock and elsewhere in Scotland who either went into private enterprise or obtained coalmines of their own.

His efforts were not in word only but also in deed. He would seek to equip and enable the ex-slaves to obtain a measure of security and self-sufficiency by establishing mechanisms for self and community development, as a new society was supposed to take shape; one in which he was prepared to play a part but not one which the plantocracy was prepared to allow. He founded the first Sick and Friendly Society in Trinidad in 1846 in Freetown Valley (i.e. Belmont). This movement was an incentive to savings as well as providing for financial relief in times of illness and death, (even in modern times it is found primarily among Black communities); the first public library at Greyfriars on 18th November 1842. At Arouca with the help of a second missionary Rev'd. George Brodie, there was begun a week-day school of about thirty to forty children and a class for adult females. He also founded the Trinidad branch of the British and Foreign Bible Society. Kennedy's commendation of the gospel came in no alien voice nor disguise. He was therefore able to reach others in their otherness by adopting and adapting their symbols and idiom when other churches were more ready to cut them off as non-Christian and non –inspired. He was ahead of his time in not persisting with a Eurocentric gospel, but one that had the ability to meet people at the point of their need at their particular level of existence, recognizing that each person is a full human being endowed with an intrinsic God-given dignity and the native cultural and religious tools needed to receive the Christian understanding of God in the finality of Jesus Christ.

His Covenanter background would lead him to challenge the State, in a manner of speaking. His particular Secessionist strand in the Church of Scotland's history also adhered to a principle called 'voluntaryism' which meant that it was opposed to the State's promoting one religion and giving financial aid over others. The church was supposed to support itself from among the congregational givings. No outside funding was accepted. This was also part of a theological arrogance that looked upon money given by persons outside the church as 'devil money', not fit for the kingdom of God. The government was surprised when both Kennedy and Brodie refused state aid in the grant of lands and construction of buildings for their congregations at Greyfriars', Port-of-Spain and at Arouca to its utter astonishment and dismay. Kennedy wrote, "I could on no account be a party to the mis-appropriation of funds raised for purely secular purposes...Ere they could believe such a thing possible, I had to appear at the Council Board and give my reasons for declining the proffered boon, and I may mention incidentally that something similar took place when some years later a site for the Arouca Church was bought from Government." (20). Brodie remarked, "...the price consequently determined by Government was not so low as at all to infringe upon the principle of voluntaryism." (21). These gentlemen would, no doubt, have been witness to the seemingly depraved jostling for political influence and patronage between the Roman and Anglican churches, the heavy rivalry between them for establishment of schools and 'territorial expansion' as it were by what Kennedy condemned as 'indiscriminate baptism' of adults and infants, i.e. without counselling, instruction or discipleship and sometimes without the candidates' consent.

This strict adherence to voluntaryism though would come to severely hinder the work and expansion of Scots Presbyterianism in Trinidad. But it also showed a religion that was mainly an overseas chaplaincy for Scots merchants and expatriates and one related to the established religion of a kingdom of Britain thereby carrying much weight and more respectability than the non-conformist ones as the Baptists or Methodists, not prepared to be a puppet of the State but in fact demanding of the State as an equal, its due rights and privileges. This was something neither the Roman nor the Anglican Church was prepared to do. Roman Catholicism was established as the religion of Trinidad under the Spanish and the Anglican Church under the British in 1844. In so doing one sought to covet and achieve pomp and glory as the most important church on the island and through its state connections bid for a share in imperialist expansion in money, property and greater social mobility among its adherents. Rev'd. Kennedy would not sit idly by as the Anglican Church jostled for political power and patronage at that time, eventually becoming established as the religion of Trinidad in 1844. He immediately launched a challenge to this dictatorial imposition and the arrogance of Anglicanism. (The Church of England had long claimed spiritual jurisdiction over the Church of Scotland through its see of York and even after the Reformation sought under Archbishop Laud of Canterbury et al, to reimpose episcopacy or rule by diocesan bishops and the English Prayer Book over and against Presbyterianism and the Book of Common Order, which Kennedy's Covenanter tradition fiercely and successfully opposed and defeated). Kennedy understood that while churches in Europe might be established religions of particular countries, this was primarily so because of a majority of citizens being members thereof and because of nationalist struggles and cleavings arising especially out of the Protestant Reformation as had been the case in England and Scotland.

This idea was not out of harmony with those of John Calvin the Swiss Reformer who reintroduced to the church its presbyterial government and heritage as nearly as possible. Calvin saw nothing incompatible with a State church because the civil magistrate was authorised by God as well. But Reformed principles would demand that neither the church nor the State be treated as puppets of each other, but as separate realms for the mutual welfare, spiritual and temporal, of the people respectively. Noted Scottish theologian Andrew Melville had sharply reiterated to King James VI of Scotland, in 1596, before he ascended the English throne, that, "There are two kings and two kingdoms in Scotland. There is Christ Jesus the King and His Kingdom the Kirk, whose subject King James the Sixth is, and of whose kingdom not a king, nor a lord, nor a head, but a member." (22). Hence the fact that even today while Queen Elizabeth II is temporal head of the Church of England and involved in the appointments of bishops et al, in Scotland she becomes a member of the Church of Scotland only, with no temporal or spiritual power. She also changes denomination in effect.

This particular interpretation of State and Church and the separation of their powers brought Kennedy to be the staunchest advocate against the establishment of the Church of England in Trinidad. Charismatically he organised the first and very successful ecumenical Christian meeting at Greyfriars to challenge the Anglican assumption, in October of 1844. It was attended by Presbyterians,

Methodists, Baptists and even the Roman Catholic bishop; a most outstanding achievement in Christian ecumenism for a time when rivalry, theological distrust and mutual condemnations were hostile and openly contentious; (Kennedy was once said to have openly rebuked the Anglican Rector of Trinity Cathedral, then Church, for standing and doffing his hat in salute to the Blessed Sacrament as it passed in procession during a Roman Catholic observance of Corpus Christi, which Protestants considered as idolatry and was never to be worshipped and adored but strictly eaten and drunk in Holy Communion). It was far ahead of its time and showed and promised a church united in a common cause and being able to overlook their divisions and divisiveness for the sake of a constitutional and national issue that would bring to bear on future State and Church relations both officially and psychologically. And although disestablishment would not take place for about another twenty years, the movement continued and met regularly at Greyfriars, but unfortunately after the cause was won, parties returned to their respective camps, rivalry was continued and the effort forgotten by subsequent leaders who fell back into a pre-establishment modus operandi. It was this united Christianity that should have come to the then colonised world in an apostolic engagement/encounter model and which would have served the intent of the gospel far greater than the present inheritance of divisiveness and rivalry that works against any attempt at a truly national community in spite of the heavy heterogeny and that was learnt from the empire as a means to political favour and prestige; itself a remnant of the tendencies appropriated from the centuries of Caesaropapism in the Holy Roman Empire.

Kennedy's efforts were not limited to the slavery dilemma. He welcomed the Madeiran Presbyterian Refugees in 1846 into Greyfriars until they could build a church of their own. He even learnt Portuguese so that within a month's time they would have intelligible services in their native tongue. His Reformed spirituality would no doubt have been concerned with their understanding of and response to the 'Word', but it was limited, as Reformed spirituality on the whole is, to a heavy emphasis on worship of God with the mind, that it was and is not prepared to allow the elements of sensuality and mystery apart from the intellect. He refused them Communion because they could not understand English though they protested that the actions, their faith and prior instruction in its meaning were sufficient to engender an appropriate faith response. They knew with their hearts and minds though not with their ears, but Kennedy just wanted to be sure. Churches of the Reformed / Protestant tradition may be said to have made Jesus Christ too final in their Mediaeval attempt at purity of Christian doctrine and worship. There was no concept of the communion of saints beyond a vertical relationship among members of the church militant. It was a religion stripped and 'purified' of the 'elohim', with no saints, spirits, jumbies or communion of saints with the church triumphant. There was a general denial and lack of any appreciation of the 'Mysterious', only an insistence on obedience to the moral law without any warmth of soul or imagination. Kennedy's strict Calvinism precluded this, because faith comes by a literal hearing of the ear and mind, whereas a more catholic understanding would prefer that one's faith grasps with the heart and imagination first and then with the mind, as when the Mass was celebrated exclusively in Latin, then being a vastly unknown tongue. Against Kennedy's action, the Refugees protested vehemently, claiming that they fully knew and understood in their minds as well as their hearts and their faith what the celebration meant and thus language was secondary, if of no point at all. Communion with Christ and his church was of ultimate concern no matter how attained. But Kennedy was adamant, and they were debarred from communion until a Portuguese minister could be procured some months later. In this regard Paul Tillich would say, "The general criticism of the Roman Church by all Protestant groups was the exclusion of the prophetic self-criticism by the authoritarian system of the Church and the growth of the sacramental elements of faith over the moral-personal ones…The break (with Rome) also brought about a loss of Roman sacramentalism and the unity based on them. In consequence of this loss, Protestantism became more and more representative of the moral type of ultimate concern. In this way it lost not only the large number of ritual traditions in the

Catholic churches but also a full understanding of the presence of the holy in sacramental and mystical experiences." (23).

He would also come to attack the system of indentured labour of East Indians as well through the Anti-Slavery Society. He described the system as being, "...impolitic, unjust and inhuman—destined ere long to create a human pen instead of a Paradise as it might be." (24). But time was running out for this forerunner of Liberation Theology. He vehemently contended with the feudal order and became virtually alone, a voice crying in the wilderness. In one of his letters to the Foreign Mission Board he wrote, "It is true that during my residence here I have always raised my voice against any act I considered as tyrannic and oppressive and disgraceful for anyone to practice; but in doing so I did my duty and nothing else..." (25).

This remarkable, if not often controversial figure had made many enemies and lost many friends. He had the courage of his convictions in the cause of righteousness and justice as he saw it. Again he wrote, "I know that my efforts have gained me many enemies, but I pity them: and I am quite satisfied with the small number of true friends I leave here." (26). In 1849 Alexander Kennedy contracted Yellow Fever and was so weakened he could not even stand up. He resigned his charge, served a few months at Arouca and later left these shores. He stopped in the USA and Canada calling on friends and relatives on the way home to Scotland. It has long been assumed that in Canada's cooler climate his health improved so dramatically that he remained there for another forty-two years in ministerial service almost up to his death in 1892; but W. Wood observes, "But on reaching Canada he found wide doors of opportunity for service and cast in his lot with the church in Upper Canada for whatever years of labor might remain to him." (27). Either he had been cured of the Yellow Fever by the time he arrived there or he used it as a convenient ruse to get out of Trinidad whose doors were closing or already closed to him unlike Canada where they were 'wide open' and while he had the opportunity to do so.

His Trinidad ministerial colleagues paid tribute to him in an appropriate valedictory address which said inter alia, "As a constant, zealous and uncompromising advocate of human rights, the remembrance of your name will long continue to prove as refreshing and delightful as 'ointment poured forth'; nor will it soon be forgotten with what decision and powerful effect you have vindicated the spiritual independence of the Church of Christ in Trinidad." (28). His contracting Yellow Fever was the excuse he needed to get out of Trinidad after having alienated his Scots congregation who as planters and merchants and tradesmen were part of the ascendancy. He no longer had a place at Greyfriars and the church would be better serviced by other ministers not so radical, and who could better accommodate the views, feelings and wishes of the imperial power. He was quite unlike John Morton and Kenneth Grant, pioneer Canadian Presbyterian missionaries among the East Indians who by their close association and financial dependence on the planters openly advocated indentureship and saw no theological or ethical problem in separating the physical human condition from the spiritual. Idris Hamid notes, "The alliance between the missionary and the planter in the Presbyterian Church may explain certain attitudes and ethical positions of the missionaries. It is an alliance that blinded the eyes of the missionaries to basic ethical issues of the era, and the particular needs of the people for whom they claimed responsibility…The early missionaries cultivated the friendship of the planters. Apart from playing golf together, they visited and socialised with each other. They also received support for the school from the planters…Not only were they contributing to the schools; that contribution also went towards the missionaries' salaries…" (29).

Kennedy stands out for the strength of his convictions that permeated the very fibre of his being and were the sum of his Christianity, his prophetic voice and pilgrim quality that marked that period with distinction but which was ultimately rejected for the status quo. But as a man ahead of his time, marked with the purity of the Christian gospel, he was effectively run out of Greyfriars and of Trinidad. He himself acknowledged the source of his convictions from the Covenanter tradition of the Scottish lowlands, as he wrote near the end of his ministry in Canada, "Many years afterwards he wrote of the grave of Alexander Peden at the 'gallowsfit,' in New Cumnock. 'That was a sacred spot to me. I loved to linger by Peden's grave...Having read with avidity and deep interest the records of the labours and sufferings of the martyr-heroes of my native land, the grave of one of those men of whom the world was not then worthy and whose memory was yet traditionally fragrant in the district could not fail to have attractions for me; and every visit to such a spot deepened my detestation of oppression, which has never waned, and fanned in me the love of liberty, both civil and religious, a feeling which has only waxed I ween as years and intimacy with the world's wickedness have increased." (30). A Canadian tribute to him mentions that he was of, "...strong mind and ever ready to defend [his] views with an abounding measure of the 'perfervidum ingenium Scotorum.'...His labours [in Port-of-Spain] were mainly among the merchants and clerks of the town, but there were also many negroes within the sphere of his ministrations. As he was the pioneer Presbyterian missionary there, on his shoulders fell the double burden of combatting established evils and of organising and establishing the forces that make for righteousness...From the beginning he set himself to seek to better the condition of the negroes and to prevent the injustices and heartless oppression from which they suffered. This naturally brought him into conflict with a certain powerful class in the colony, but he was ever ready to defend the stand he took. 1840, the Anti-Slavery Society, in recognition of his services, presented him with an address and a snuff-box...For fourteen years, amid many discouragements and hindrances, Mr. Kennedy gave himself to arduous work in Port-of-Spain. " (31). Such discouragements and hindrances dogged his ministry here from beginning to end, and his zeal 'for the Lord's house' was his driving force. But alas, then physically weakened by Yellow Fever, he no longer had the physical strength needed to support his spirituality for him to continue. As a lone figure, a man ahead of his time, he has gone the way of forgotten heroes, overshadowed and overlooked by the prevailing sentiments of his time, awaiting perhaps, like his mortal frame, a future deserved resurrection; like the Elijah of the Old Testament returning to herald Messiah's coming; a prophet to sound the reawakening call to Reformed Christianity in post-colonial Trinidad and Tobago. He commends to the modern society the spirituality not only of a Liberator God but also of the Suffering Servant; cut off from the land of the living; persecuted, despised and rejected. A spirituality that needs to be recaptured to deal with the cleavings of a society in an identity struggle.

He arrived here on 25th January and if Presbyterians are to appreciate better their emphasis on predestination and divine ordering of human affairs, the date marks the Feast of the Conversion of St. Paul. Here was a prophet, an evangelist, a preacher, a pastor; one who was persecuted and run out of cities, who challenged the ruling authorities; thus Kennedy stood spiritually in the apostolic succession of Paul himself. For the Reformed tradition, this apostolic succession does not consist primarily in a physical, historical line of ordination traceable back to the apostles, but while ordination is 'handed down' this succession is seen mainly in terms of faithfulness to the apostolic deposit of faith and teaching. When the church declares in the Nicene Creed its belief in the 'Apostolic Church', it is a church sent in every age and generation through the ordained ministry with the apostolic witness of ministry. In this regard it can be said then that the church of the colonial era was not an apostolic church as it had lost that model of engagement/encounter, its apostolic ethic, witness, preaching and tools of evangelising others, and exchanged them for a distorted one dictated by the lust for earthly empire and glory at the expense of the human condition.

Kennedy was also providentially ordained in and sent by Greyfriars' Church of Glasgow, Scotland, for whom he named the Port-of-Spain congregation. It was built on the site of an old Greyfriars' monastery, whose monks were the followers of the rule of St. Francis of Assisi, and have been so called because of their grey habit. These men of piety and sound theological learning established churches, monasteries and universities throughout Europe under a divine call of Francis to rebuild God's church from moral and academic decay. The Greyfriars settled in towns in the meanest and poorest quarters and even among lepers and other outcasts, under a strict vow of poverty. Eric Kirton remarks, "The Friars in Scotland maintained the tradition of the order. The Dundee Friars criticised the existing order and in 1528 preached against the licentious lives of the Bishops and against the abuse of cursing...Such people who disagreed with and rejected the faith as enunciated by Mother Church were denounced as heretics...Edinburgh burnt its heretics who had been accused and tried and convicted as a salutary lesson to those such as the Friars of Stirling who dared to criticise the abuse of excommunication, the financial rapacity and the immoral lives of churchmen." (32). So that in this regard Kennedy could be said to have stood spiritually in the order of the Greyfriars, in whose monastic surroundings he was ordained and sent (an apostle is one who is 'sent'), because of his radical theology, conviction and praxis.

What of that radical prophetic call today; a call back to our apostolic roots? Hugh Cameron in his tribute to Alexander Kennedy asks the pertinent question in looking at Kennedy's contribution to Trinidad and Tobago and the church there, "In so doing, we must examine our own consciences and answer the question whether Kennedy would be satisfied today that we have been true and faithful stewards and, indeed, disciples of that missionary call and purpose upon which he was sent and for which he struggled in mind and body and in spirit with great tribulation at sacrifice of his own health..." (33). Greyfriars' of Port-of-Spain and through its influence, the Church of Scotland in Trinidad, rejected Alexander Kennedy and has continued to reject any resemblance to his polemics because that is not the kind of church they have ever, always wanted to be from the start. Their church is an ideal one catering to the interests of a neo-colonialist, europeanised upper class in an effort to maintain the pre-independence mindset against the rest of the society and the Church of Christ. It has refused to engage in any attempt or struggle towards selfhood, self-determination and national identity. It is the dying relict of a truly colonial church.

With the departure of Kennedy and its subsequent association with the Canadian missionaries in the Presbytery of Trinidad, i.e. Morton, Grant et al, the church renewed its colonial flavour in its regard to local ministry. A comparison may be made between Kennedy's polemic against the introduction of East Indian indentured labour in 1845 and against oppression in general with the sentiments of a later minister of St. Ann's Church, Rev'd. Gilbert Earle, of Canadian origin, in regard to the atrocities in Amritsar, India in 1919, as Sitahal notes, "Rev. Gilbert Earle a Canadian from New Brunswick who was editor of the 'Trinidad Presbyterian' [magazine] …thought it worthwhile to comment favourably on repressive action taken by Brigadier-General R.E.M. Dyer in Amritsar, India, on April 10, 1919. General Dyer had ordered his men to fire on an unarmed gathering obviously in reprisal to the killing of a few Englishmen some days before. He exhausted his ammunition on the crowd, killing between four or five hundred and wounding fifteen hundred. Rev. Earle comments in the 'Trinidad Presbyterian', 'He meant to punish those who had disobeyed and give them a lesson'. He further stated that Dyer had rendered useful service not only to the Empire but to the Indians as well. Highly unmoved by the cause of Indian independence and fully aware of the thousands of East Indians in Trinidad he went on to conclude, 'The leniency of British rule is proverbial, but it is sometimes misunderstood, and the Amritsar incident will be a useful reminder that the pastime of twisting the Lion's tail has its dangers." (34). How remarkable to see that the church lost the prophetic voice with which it first announced its presence, with so much promise for the future. It was no longer the church that Kennedy built for God, and St. Ann's was no longer the beacon of refuge and hope as it had been for its founders, the Madeiran refugees or exiles as they are also known, who found rest from oppression and persecution, when this polemic would ring from the heart, mind and hand of one of its later pastors and no doubt from its pulpit too.

There was, however, a nationalist feeling mainly in Sangre Grande but also in Arouca, and a desire to be part of the self-seeking that was cleaving the other side of Presbyterianism in the island as well being influenced by the Garveyism sweeping the African diaspora but not limited to it since it would also influence other oppressed peoples here and the world over. Rev'd. William Henry Mayhew had been a Barbadian immigrant coming here in the wave of particularly Barbadian but also other West Indian immigration to Trinidad from the 1880's onward. He had been a teacher of the Moravian church and, living in Ste. Madeleine aligned himself to the Presbyterian cause since it was the nearest thing to his denomination. He became catechist under Rev'd. John Smith Wilson and was instrumental in the establishment of the Ste. Madeleine congregation (now Methodist) and the Marabella church (now Presbyterian). After a period of study in the United States he was ordained by the local presbytery in 1902. After the dedication of the Sangre Grande church in 1904, Mayhew was translated from San Fernando to the eastern town as missionary and served until 1912 when he returned to the USA to pursue doctoral studies where he encountered Garveyism which his former mentor, J. S. Wilson, in typical white fashion, condemned as a brand of communism (35). He later aligned himself with the African Methodist Episcopal cause as its pioneer missionary to Trinidad, chiefly identifying with its cause of African selfhood which the Church of Scotland was not prepared tolerate or engage in. It had turned its back on Kennedy's engagement polemic with the oppressed in their suffering and cause for liberation and self-identity and was concretising into a primary beacon of European zenith of colonial Christianity.

Several decades later in 1928 another Barbadian now, James Worrell, of Methodist stock would be appointed catechist and later ordained minister in 1932, to Sangre Grande to rescue a dying congregation, financially and numerically because of economic stringency and population shifts to urban areas as a result of the fall in cocoa prices and, the cessation of funding from Scotland, both in 1925. Sangre Grande/Manzanilla was a thriving centre of cocoa plantations in the east. Worrell was not content to remain silent in the light of the blatant discrepancies between the treatment of Scottish expatriate ministers and local ones. But the major problem for the Scottish Mission Council as had been for the Canadian one was the inability of the expatriate ministers to reconcile their membership of the parent denomination with that of the local ministers who belonged to a local, federated presbytery and not, in fact, ministers of the parent denomination. They were ministers of the local church and subject to local presbytery decisions whereas the expatriates were of the parent church and subject to the better conditions afforded from there. Worrell would also adopt the prophetic voice of Rev'd. Kennedy, for whom his Manzanilla church was named, and become involved in the Labour movement's call for better working conditions for lower wage earners and those in the oil, sugar and other industries. Worrell spoke on many a political and labour platform in the mid 1930's. In so doing he alienated much of his white plantation following in Sangre Grande, as did Kennedy at Greyfriars some one hundred years ago exactly. Worrell, like Kennedy, spoke his mind and found himself in trouble. He was alienating Greyfriars as well, which had been Sangre Grande's saviour during its financial crisis. That was never the way a church or its minister should behave. They were too sanitised for that. Worrell subsequently resigned in 1947, a very disenchanted and disillusioned man of God, having paid the sacrificial price of the prophets. When he left, however, the congregation mostly left with him, joining other churches more in line with the trend of selfhood that was sweeping the country then. Only three members remained by the time Rev'd. A. N. MacKean of Greyfriars assumed joint charge of Sangre Grande.

At Arouca, Rev'd. Felix Barrow adopted a more tacit but equally prophetic approach. He was never a forceful preacher but he used his other gifts and abilities in this movement for selfhood as well. He opened up his relatively well-read, personal library to the young people of the district. He also sought to empower them in music, art, drama and debating, of which his church hall was the hub. The Literary and Debating Club and the Social and Cultural Club were just two of the more continuing areas of his ministry in which he sought to empower the rising young generation of nationals, not only of his congregation but of the parish in general. He thus saw the intrinsic worth and value of every human being without enforcing the traditional bar expected at the time of Christian religious persuasion. His vision was one of wholeness for the total human being, not just for the soul, and of a new and redeemed way of life for whole community. His annual missionary meetings had invited guest speakers of the likes of Captain Arthur Cipriani, labour leader and agitator of workers' rights, H. O. B. Wooding who was Trinidad and Tobago's first local Chief Justice and George Padmore, a fellow Aroucan with whom he had a close friendship, and who was a pivotal figure in the Marcus Garvey Pan African movement. Barrow was an educator and ex-officio manager of the Arouca Government School. He saw education as the key to empowerment on the way to being adequately equipped and self-sufficient. At that time the emphasis was not primarily on African cultural, racial and religious identity as in the post-independence era, but concentrated chiefly on the attainment of self-determination, self-government and eventually independence. It was about the rights of local citizens to have access to all institutions and resources of the state and to be regarded as first class citizens in every regard. It was about the ends of colonialism and the age of independence.

Mayhew, Barrow and Worrell can be said to have built on the foundations of the Rev'd. William Fraser Dickson, who had established and for many years chaired the Arouca branch of the Pan-African Association, [which had even received lectures by another famous local Pan-Africanist and son of Arouca soil, Henry Sylvester Williams, of whom he was also a very close friend] (36), and in communion with those sentiments and ideas that would have been brought by the African-American ministers who came during the second and third decades of the twentieth century. Indeed as early as the end of the nineteenth century the Church of Scotland in Trinidad among its Black clergy was not out of sync with the urgings of the rest of society. It was, therefore, seeking to build on the precepts of its pioneer minister, Alexander Kennedy in rooting the church and having it identify with the local landscape rather than being an overseas chaplaincy to a colony of persons with a rootedness in another country, albeit a colonial power, or the provenance of only one racial and / or economic grouping.

There has always been the thought in Greyfriars/St. Ann's that the church should not engage in politics and hence maintain the dichotomy between spiritual and temporal. This has also been a pertinent reason for not wanting to join with the Presbyterian church, whose local leadership had developed a strong prophetic voice in Parliament and in protest, (like the Black Power Movement in 1970), in the struggles of their subjugated peoples for basic human rights, justice and dignity. Even the church's system of parochial government reflected this thinking in the separation of temporal affairs as property and finance run by the deacons or board of managers, and spiritual affairs run by the elders, with the minister over all as the parochial bishop; (after all Presbyterianism is also episcopacy at a parish rather than a diocesan or national level and all bishops corporately rather than individually at district and national levels). And yet this way of thinking is strange to the essence of Reformed spirituality which espouses a strong social ethic and world-engaged way of being, rooted in the conviction that God is sovereign over all of life. It becomes scandalous to people who are dying daily of poverty, violence and oppression if we merely spiritualise their sufferings with the opiate gospel and fail to identify and attempt to root out the cause of the evil; because that would mean baring their souls and getting one's hands dirty by "eating and drinking with sinners". The church would rather prefer a second-hand method of participation and engagement, by giving to a charitable cause or organisation as the Salvation Army rather than get dirty itself. The true essence of Reformed spirituality can be seen when the World Alliance of Reformed Churches (Presbyterian and Congregational) dismissed the South African member churches for their complicity in the evil system of apartheid because, "You did not so learn Christ." Eph. 4:20. H. Russel Botman of the Uniting Reformed Church in Southern Africa goes further to state, "To affirm a doctrinal statement that relinquishes the 'doctrinal' connection between justice and justification would be a betrayal of everything that Christianity has learned about justification after Auschwitz and apartheid." (37).

The church had never really focussed on schools and other social outreach programmes because of the culture of voluntaryism, which while good theoretically, is economically disastrous for church expansion schemes. The church therefore rejected Government's financial assistance, though it later accepted the Ecclesiastical Grant; which was thirty dollars in 1908; and which was not really much and went chiefly to pay the salaries of the ministers of the weaker congregations. A controversy arose back then in 1908 over the acceptance of state aid for church work, namely a school that was begun by the Sangre Grande mission in Plum Road. The Hon. George Goodwille who had made his mark in public life and on the Legislative Council withdrew his eldership and even church membership since he believed the church had departed from its hallowed standards. The church knew better that its work could not survive on meagre church funds alone; but Goodwille's sentiments and prestige prevailed and State aid was refused. The church later handed over the work to the Presbyterian church as it could not cope financially or otherwise as time would tell. There has always been the feeling that because of the many 'good men' of societal standing and influence, the church would not want to lose their support and its association with their prestigious name that it would compromise anything to retain such people, even at the sacrifice of common sense, practical theology and persons holding these sincere convictions; even as Alexander Kennedy was sacrificed because the church wanted to develop and portray a particular image and standing in the public eye.

There is no vision, no planning, no liberation theology and praxis. An attempt to deal with the vagrancy problem on the literal doorstep of Greyfriars is met with the resolution to drive them away by wetting the pavements. And local ministers are coerced into giving tacit approval because it is not ministerial-like to trouble the waters if one knows where one's bread is buttered! There is no protest in this passive church, so there can be no grace of the gospel given an opportunity to release its intrinsic power. It has lost the prophetic voice and pilgrim quality of its founder. It has a considerable amount of money albeit; legacies from the merchants of old, who once commanded most of Frederick Street, Port-of-Spain. But it has no zeal or imagination to put that money to serious Christian outreach. Money is always used to make good investment returns, never to be risked on peoples' salvation.

Scotland has been afraid to let the church go on its own fearing that the colonial mindset and lack of succession planning would eventually annihilate the body. The local church is concerned that any union with the Presbyterian Church would make it lose whatever identity it believes it has, remembering that church's own internal struggles for selfhood, as well as the many financial, lifestyle and other scandals and challenges the Presbyterian Church has been having throughout its history. There was always the fact that the Presbyterian Church is composed of at least 95% East Indians and there would be racial imbalances and distrust that have their roots deep in the history of this land and are not easily erased or dealt with. This racial separation and subsequent distrust could have been avoided were it not for the policy of both Scottish and Canadian Mission Councils. It is well-known that the Canadian Mission under Morton insisted on a separate mission to the East Indian because they saw Christianity as an African dominated religion, and who were already not attending the government ward schools because of racial antipathies. And though there have been several instances of both these Mission Councils sharing buildings of the Scottish Mission Council, as in Marabella, Arima and Arouca, for services and other related activities; there were always two services right up until the 1960's. The morning service was for the Scots, African worshippers to whom it primarily directed its work, and the afternoon one for the Canadian Mission East Indians.

In the early days this was necessitated moreso by a language barrier as the East Indians had their services done in Hindi, which would have been a bit chaotic and awkward were it fused with an English one. But this separation continued long after these latter meetings were using English too. In any event the Scottish services were perceived to be more aesthetic than the East Indian ones since by then the African was more culturally and academically adapted to a Western urban or semi-urban way of being; a mode into which the East Indian was only lately being introduced, and who still would have retained much of one's peasantness, owing to the lower living conditions of the indentured system. This perception has remained today with the Church of Scotland seen as urban-based and the Presbyterian Church as more rural through the geographic setting of the various congregations and the historical realities and biases associated with them.

A union or association with the Presbyterian Church, however, would mean a whole new drama of cleavings that no one really has the energy to engage in having been quite drained in the independence and other concomitant struggles then and thereafter. If the local

Church of Scotland were to unite with the Presbyterian church, it would have to own the struggles of that church. But this comes too late as there could have been one struggle and hence one identity and one true sense of unity and marriage from at least 1891, if not before. There was no Trinidad consciousness then. The church had a concern as to which expatriate colonial group one belonged, and because the presbytery was not recognised in Scotland it was felt that a Canadian church would not sit well with one's Scottishness. Any attempt at a marriage of these two churches must not be out of convenience or a necessity for survival or merely for local self-determination. It would then not be a marriage but a takeover, which the local Church of Scotland fears. But it must entail either an owning of the Presbyterian church's selfhood and the struggles that brought it there, or the bringing to the marriage bed its own selfhood as a full and equal partner.

And the Church of Scotland in Trinidad has no selfhood, though it could if it really wanted to. It has never had the concerted cleavings as other local Christian bodies for this selfhood because it has always seen itself as a chaplaincy of the Church of Scotland. It is, in essence, stuck in time, hence anachronistic. Like Charles Dickens', Miss Havisham (from the novel, Great Expectations), in her wedding dress, unremoved years after her being jilted at the altar, the church is stuck in the time, mode and mindset of Rev'd. A. N. MacKean's era, 1947-1969, its heyday with overflowing pews, a nationally renowned Sunday school and an erudite preacher and pastor. How the old folks remember and relive those good old days and long for their return! With Lot's wife they look back and stultify and soon die. They fail to see that they no longer have any national or community significance or relevance and that their churches are virtually empty. They are a closed community; a church existing for itself and by itself, selfishly clinging on to its few remaining mega assets, real and financial. They have been closing down their churches one by one, and sooner or later none will be left unless a radical reformation takes place which embraces the return of Alexander Kennedy and his spirituality, in a latter day prophet to revive this organism of Christ's body.

NOTES

1. 45. Hugh Cameron, Tribute to Rev. Alexander Kennedy at Anniversary Service to mark the 150th anniversary of his arrival, Greyfriars' Church, Port-of-Spain, Trinidad W. I. 26th January 1986.
2. Ibid.
3. Harold Sitahal, Re-thinking Mission for the Caribbean, published in: Out of the Depths pg. 34; Ed. Idris Hamid © 1977.
4. Letters of David McCowan from Trinidad to Scotland 1800-1834, collected by Bruce McCowan, Gr-Gr-Gr-Gr-Nephew, for the James McCowan Memorial Social History Society, Ontario, Canada.
5. Greyfriars of Trinidad 1837-1987, published by the Kirk Session of Greyfriars' / St. Ann's Church of Scotland, 1987, ch. 1, The Beginning, pg. 10.
6. Op. Cit. no. 1
7. Ibid.
8. Maureen Warner Lewis, Guinea's Other Suns—The African Dynamic in Trinidad Culture, ch. 2, Africans in 19th Century Trinidad, pg. 23; The Majority Press, Dover Mass. USA © 1991.
9. Op. Cit. no. 1
10. Op. Cit. no. 3, pg. 23
11. Idris Hamid, A History of the Presbyterian Church in Trinidad 1868-1968; The Struggles of a Church in Colonial Captivity, ch. 3 Leadership Development pg. 129.
12. Selwyn Cudjoe, Beyond Boundaries: The Intellectual Tradition in Nineteenth Century Trinidad, ch. 5, The Jammetization of the Culture 1838-1851, pg. 367: Calaloux Publications © 2003
13. Op. Cit. no. 1

14. Frederick Hilborn Talbot, African American Worship—New Eyes for Seeing, ch. 3, Towards a Theology of Worship—Human Responses to Divine Encounters; Preaching, pg. 68; © 1998.
15. Port-of-Spain Gazette, editorial, August 3, 1838.
16. Op. Cit. no. 5 pg. 12
17. Ibid.
18. 60. Eric Kirton, Greyfriars of Trinidad, preparatory paper 1986, pg. 5.
19. Op. Cit. no. 5, pg. 12
20. Op. Cit. no. 1
21. Ibid.
22. John H. S. Burleigh, A Church History of Scotland, Pt. 3, Reformation, sect. 3, Church and State Under James the Sixth, 1567-1625, pg. 205; Op. cit. no. 45. Oxford University Press, © 1960.
23. Op. Cit. no. 3
24. Op. Cit. no. 22
25. Ibid.
26. W. Wood, Past Years in Pickering, pg. 74.
27. Op. Cit. no. 5, pg. 13
28. Op. Cit. no. 11, ch. 1 The Historical Experience, pg. 46.
29. Op. Cit. no. 26, pg. 71/2.
30. Ibid.
31. Op. Cit. no. 5 pg. 2
32. Op. Cit. no. 1
33. Op. Cit. no. 3, pg. 41
34. Ibid. pg. 115
35. The History of Barrow Memorial Church of Scotland, Arouca Trinidad W. I., 1840-2002, pt. 2 God is Working His Purpose Out, pg. 11.; ed. Clifford Rawlins.
36. O. Cit. no. 11, ch. 4, The Struggle for Selfhood, pg. 150.
37. 83. H. Russel Botman, Should the Reformed Join In? published in Reformed World, theological journal of the World Alliance of Reformed Churches, Geneva, Switzerland, Volume 52, No. 1, March 2002, pg. 15, Reformed Reflections on the Joint Declaration on the Doctrine of Justification.

A SHORT PAPER PRESENTED AT A PANEL DISCUSSION, "LET'S TALK CANNABIS: PERSPECTIVES FOR LEGALISATION" AT THE CIPRIANI COLLEGE OF LABOUR AND CO-OPERATIVE STUDIES, VALSAYN CAMPUS, ON WEDNESDAY 21ST NOVEMBER 2018

Chair, distinguished panellists and fellow speakers, other distinguished guests, members of the media, ladies and gentlemen: Grace, mercy, and peace be with you all.

I wish to thank the organisers for reposing in me the confidence to share with you some thoughts from a biblical and theological perspective on the use of cannabis and any possible decriminalisation or legalisation of the plant and its uses.

Many Christians use the scriptures of the Old and New Testaments as the supreme rule of faith and life and so would want to see if the Bible says anything about marijuana or the use of such drugs. The Bible, for example, says nothing about tobacco or tobacco use because that was not part of Middle Eastern landscape in which the scriptures are set. There was a time when tobacco use was widely accepted and commended, having been one of the prizes of European colonisation of the Americas. Indeed, the first Presbyterian Minister in Trinidad, the Rev'd. Alexander Kennedy received a snuff box from his wider ministerial colleagues as a parting gift when he left these shores in 1849. And while the Bible knows nothing about tobacco, its detrimental effects to health are now universally acknowledged, and people are wont to quote scriptural texts about the body as the temple of the Holy Spirit, but one hundred and fifty years ago they did not see it that way. Human reason, science, and medical research have come into play here.

In the same way, there are texts that refer to a prohibition on drunkenness, and some would even go further to ban alcohol altogether and cannot even fathom that our Lord actually turned water into some of the best wine ever made, but would rather fool themselves and the unsuspecting and say he made grape juice, in order to preserve some sense of sinlessness to Jesus as if alcohol in and of itself is a sin. And yet the book of Esther talks about the feast of Purim; a time when Jews get purposefully drunk to celebrate their deliverance from genocide through the machinations of that book's protagonist.

It is the same with cannabis. Is it mentioned in the Bible? It is believed that the word commonly translated hemp in modern translations and calamus in the old King James' Version is the word, "kaneh-bosm", kaneh, meaning reed, and bosm, aromatic, and one can perhaps see a linguistic evolution in pronunciation from "kaneh-bosm" to cannabis. It is said of hemp that it was used as an ingredient in making the anointing oil of the Temple particularly, and that an herb bearing its own seed is good for human use. Genesis, Ezekiel, and Revelation talk about herbs for human use and the healing of the nations but does not specify which herb, although our Rastafarian brethren would have us believe that it is marijuana in particular referred to therein.

The Bible speaks with many voices and sometimes with no voice on many issues but one thing we can affirm: God is said to have called all of his creation good, and marijuana / cannabis as part of God's creation is therefore, intrinsically good, created and redeemed in the new creation moreso in Jesus Christ. Unfortunately the irresponsible misuse of this aspect of creation has become such a risk to human health and well-being that the very plant has been called evil in se: plants such as tobacco, marijuana, coca, and the poppy of Europe and the Middle East that were once used for healing, surviving cold mountain temperatures, and long days without food, and for invoking the gods have now been given an evil and destructive connotation. How could that which was created as good by a benevolent Creator be called evil unless its use has been turned for evil instead of good? The answer lies as it does in respect of all the gifts given by the Creator in the wrong and misapplied use of the creation by deviant human behaviour, when that creation is not meant to hurt, destroy, or rob humankind of their intrinsic dignity. The modern drug culture has been built on the concept of Empire. As long as there is inordinate desire for economic wealth and power, there will always be the misuse of creation. Thus it is human behaviour that has to become responsible, not in the demonising of a plant.

We proudly display our poppies every November in remembrance of those who died in World Wars 1 and 2, in "Flanders Fields where poppies grow", and we make poppy seed buns and breads and cakes. Yet I experienced a young man in one of my former congregations accosted by a church elder for wearing a chain with a marijuana leaf pendant. And heroin is worse than anything marijuana can produce. Herein we see the hypocrisy but also the ignorance and the unfairness.

Thus our call is to restore the intrinsic justice and integrity of God's creation and our human wise and responsible use thereof. Now, I will be a little provocative here, as is my theological bent, and suggest that apart from harnessing the medical and other benefits of these plants, is there some way that tobacco and marijuana leaves could once again be used as incense in worship as they were in times past? It sounds preposterous even to think of it! But our very abhorrence of the notion just goes to demonstrate how much we have come to view these things as evil in themselves, when they are endowed with intrinsic goodness by their Creator who created all things good, Gen. 1:12. Their uses have been multifarious and widespread throughout the Americas and the Middle East for centuries. They were also used in connexion with the invocation of the gods in the mystical mixture of fire and air producing smoke. But their sacred use has been profaned by the spirit of empire solely for self-indulgent pleasure and money, and now they have become a means of our dis-ease. In their pure nature they might very well prove again to be a fragrant offering to God, whereas in their demonised and tormented state, mixed with other unnatural chemicals unfit for human consumption, they have become death producing instead of the life-giving, healing herbs they were originally created to be. The use of incense though, has always been regarded in ancient religions, as potent to attract spirits and repel others depending on the good or evil intention of the devotee, not to mention the particular type of incense used to invoke the particular deity and/or spirit.

In closing, the trees of Revelation 22:2 for the healing of the nations, especially those of tobacco, marijuana, and coca must be restored to their original life-giving and life-enhancing, God-invoking purposes; with which they were created and called good in the Beginning; for there was no death neither shall they hurt or destroy in all God's holy mountain. I thank you.

HOMILY DELIVERED AT AN ECUMENICAL ADVENT VESPERS TO LAUNCH THE CARIBBEAN COUNCIL OF CHURCHES' CENTRE FOR ECUMENICAL ENCOUNTER AND DIALOGUE AT THE ABBEY CHURCH OF OUR LADY OF THE EXILE, MOUNT ST. BENEDICT, ST. AUGUSTINE, TRINIDAD W.I. TUESDAY 9TH DECEMBER 2014 EPHESIANS 4:1-16

The word 'ecumenical' conjures up for many people the notion of churches bent solely on achieving full visible unity in the Body of Christ. And while that may be valid, it does not give force to the full meaning of the term which in the original Greek refers to, the whole inhabited earth, or as I prefer to have it, the whole created order, and not just the Christian Church. It is used fourteen times in the New Testament and in most cases is translated simply as 'world'. Ecumenism, therefore, must focus on God's love for the world in the coming of his only-begotten Son that we might have life through him. Church encounter, dialogue and unity must be grasped and shaped by this love of God for the whole created order so as to evoke and urge God's will for the unity of the world in justice, truth and peace, seeking to become God's people in the world, to the world and for the world.

    Our text this evening from Ephesians 4, exhorts us to the unity of the Spirit in the bond of peace; to grow up into Christ and become mature. Indeed the Apostle Paul, St. Peter and the writer of the letter to the Hebrews all encourage us to move from infancy and feeding on milk to maturity and strong meat. Ephesians 4:14: "We must no longer be children, tossed to and fro and blown about by every wind of doctrine, by people's trickery, by their craftiness in deceitful scheming. 15 But speaking the truth in love, we must grow up in every way into him who is the head, into Christ, 16 from whom the whole body, joined and knit together by every ligament with which it is equipped, as each part is working properly, promotes the body's growth in building itself up in love." This is the ecumenical challenge.

When I was a boy, growing up in the then fairly rural district of Arouca; a time when there were no walls or fences between neighbours, I always chanced to see a common curiosity of those more idyllic times: a paint tin or biscuit tin, or a pan as we used to call it, placed on the main stem of a growing tree so as to stunt its growth from becoming too tall and its fruit unreachable in those utter heights. Ecumenism in Trinidad and Tobago, more particularly, has experienced such stunted growth. We've been down this road before, haven't we?

In October 1844, The Rev'd. Alexander Kennedy, founder of the now defunct Greyfriars' Church and first Presbyterian missionary to this island, organised the first and very successful ecumenical Christian meeting at Greyfriars' to challenge the Anglican assumption of being the established religion of Trinidad. It was attended by Presbyterians, Methodists, Baptists and even the Roman Catholic bishop; a most outstanding achievement in Christian ecumenism for a time when rivalry, theological distrust and mutual condemnation were hostile and openly contentious. In Tobago, in 1872, there was an agreement which saw the Church of Scotland hand over its congregations to the other established church of Britain, the Church of England and had the Methodists agree to evangelise the north-eastern part of the island and the Moravians the south-western part, and neither of the three would interfere with the work of the other.

There was a National Sunday School Association and Examination that ran across denominations until the 1960's. We had collaboration in Christian Education of our young people in the Caribbean Christian Living Series in the 1950's and later the Fashion Me A People Series up until the 1980's. Time was when the Ministers of the downtown Port-of-Spain Protestant churches readily supplied one another's pulpits when one of them was on furlough and they also directly participated in the induction services of one another. What of CEPAC, CELTC, CONTACT? The bastardisation of the Diego Martin United Church by its founding denominations? The failed attempt at Church unity between the Methodists and Anglicans at the end of the 1970's? And the list can continue further. We have started and stopped, started and stopped. Where could we have been if we had continued?

That first ecumenical meeting in Greyfriars' Church in 1844, was not so much to promote Christian unity as it was to protest the establishment of one religion, as it were, over others. As such, for all the good it promoted, it nevertheless showed the rivalry which has characterised Christianity on the local landscape. The Faith that came to these parts was not the Apostolic model that urged Europe into modernity but, a fragmented group of rivals with an arrogant 'theologia gloriae', acting as pawns and instruments of Empire. With many challenging social issues facing the body of Christ today, Christianity is fragmenting more and more into ideological sectarianism, into conservative, and / or moral religious right and the liberal left. Upon hearing of a major denomination's hosting a Lenten crusade-type service not far from my church, I remarked to a senior cleric and colleague of mine that we could have been invited as a show of Christian solidarity. To that the reverend gentleman replied, *"My brother, the church is looking for members not neighbours!"* He said this not to tell me off, but to awaken me to the stark reality of the church's focus in today's society. We have all been losing members, so the emphasis is now on fighting off rivals and grabbing as many souls for Christ and beefing up our numbers to make some show that we are somehow evangelising for the Kingdom. This has been our primary downfall as we continue to rival one another for some sort of national hegemony and state patronage. Where was the united and prophetic Christian voice in last week's march against the rampant corruption in our land; that call for the church to be part of the human struggle for justice, truth and peace, to give that struggle courage and hope without seeking glory for itself, only the will of

God for Creation? But we will all readily join the queue for our share in the fifty-five million dollar Christmas goodie from the state!

How do we proceed from here? We are here to launch a centre for ecumenical encounter and dialogue; and rightly so, for ecumenism is primarily an encounter of and dialogue with God through the Lord Jesus Christ, the Word who became flesh, as at this time, and who lives and dwells among us still. Ephesians 4:4 "There is one body and one Spirit, just as you were called to the one hope of your calling, 5 one Lord, one faith, one baptism, 6 one God and Father of all, who is above all and through all and in all. 7 But each of us was given grace according to the measure of Christ's gift." Will this be another venture we start only to stop in few years hence? In our worship and prayer, as we are doing here this evening, we must all seek to encounter the resurrected Christ together, who alone can build up his church for its life and mission, through the gifts of the Spirit which he disperses among God's people. Ephesians 4:11 *"The gifts he gave were that some would be apostles, some prophets, some evangelists, some pastors and teachers, 12 to equip the saints for the work of ministry, for building up the body of Christ, 13 until all of us come to the unity of the faith and of the knowledge of the Son of God, to maturity, to the measure of the full stature of Christ."*

We must ensure therefore, that ecumenism is not acted out of personality and personal friendships we make across denominational borders. I know of a Minister who remarked that ecumenism was not "his cup of tea," and so withdrew his church from all active engagement in this regard. We ought to pray to be given the gift of unity as well as to work for it. Because, while the church is spiritually born from above, it naturally grows from below, and must be built up, each limb and organ, each cell and tissue into the life of the body of Christ, and to grow up into him, becoming equipped with ever increasing maturity, for the task of encountering, dialoguing with and renewing the created order. As the express will of the Lord Jesus for his church, ecumenism ought to be everybody's business and the church's priority, not a back burner issue as we have had it. We must encounter and dialogue with each other in each other's otherness and learn to appreciate the variety of gifts and oneness of the Spirit, not just within and among our own denominations, but of each other's denomination also. Thus this newly created space this evening ought to become a place of hospitality, a truly welcoming place, as St. Columba would put it.

The aim of this newly created space today ought to encourage the weaving together of the separated strands of Christianity, to encourage models of healing national, regional, racial and denominational and individual histories and thus, within the vision of the new and redeemed humanity in Christ, to raise up a new people of prophetic grace and pilgrim quality.

To believe in God the Father, is necessarily to believe that someone is in charge, who sees the whole picture and who is calling the whole created order back to his vision and will for it. To believe in the Lord Jesus Christ is to believe that God has encountered and dialogued with humanity and calls a church into being where all can encounter and dialogue with the risen Christ and with one another and be empowered to live his resurrection life: his body no longer broken as on the cross, but reunited, re-membered into one whole. To believe in the Holy Spirit is to believe that people can find resources beyond themselves, beyond all expectation, and sprout new and surprising capacities as to what they can achieve and accomplish, urging creation into the new and redeemed order; thus making every effort to maintain the unity of the Spirit in the very bond of peace.

May the God of peace who brought again from the dead our Lord Jesus Christ, that great shepherd of the sheep, through the blood of the eternal covenant, make us perfect in every good work to do his will; working in us that which is well-pleasing in his sight; through Jesus Christ our Lord, who with the Father and the Holy Spirit be ascribed all glory and dominion, might, majesty and praise, now and always. +Amen.

Let us pray, "Lord God, whose Son was content to die to bring new life, have mercy on your church which will do anything you ask, anything at all: except die and be reborn. Lord Christ, forbid us unity which leaves us where we are: welded into one company but extracted from the battle; engaged to be yours but not found at your side. Holy Spirit of God—reach deeper than our inertia and fears: release us into the freedom of the children of God. Amen." *Rev'd. Ian Fraser.*

CULTURAL PERSPECTIVES

These thoughts were provoked upon the killing of American missionary John Allen Chau by the Sentinelise peoples of North Sentinel Island in the Indian Ocean in early November 2018. One church elder vehemently contended that, *"The injudicious murder of a well-meaning stranger is a horrible, barbaric act of an uneducated, backward people suffering the extreme neglect of man's inhumanity to man..."* Of the following work, he had this to retort further, *"For any man to consider constructing divinely holy, righteous and perfect doctrine for our walk of faith in Jesus Christ from such a demonstration of primitive paranoia is nothing but a vile expression of intellectual vanity! I pray that it will not become the deranged whimpering of a fallen angel of light..."*

Here now is the thus described "expression of intellectual vanity."

1. The Sentinelese people are said to dwell without clothing, i.e. naked.
2. The Hebrew scriptures and Judaeo-Christian Western thought tell us that humankind became ashamed of their nakedness, in the Garden of Eden, as a result of their disobedience of God in eating the forbidden fruit, and sought to hide themselves. Thus it was necessary for God to clothe their shame by covering them with the skins of sacrificed animals, prefiguring thereby the sacrifice of Jesus in atonement for our sin and shame.
3. This is how the Jews and Christians seek to explain the generally inherent Middle Eastern shame and abhorrence of human nakedness. Greek and Roman and other ancient

religions which had no issues with human nakedness were suppressed along with everything unchristian or "pagan" when Christianity became the established religion of the Roman Empire in 318 AD. Thus the Olympic Games were banned by Christian Emperor Theodosius in the 4th century because athletes competed naked. This suppression was praised by the Church of the times.

4. If the Sentinelese have no shame about their nakedness, can it mean that they have no sin as understood in our Judaeo-Christian thinking? And if they have no sin, why do we still teach that EVERYBODY has sinned as Christians conceive it and in need of a Saviour? And so that that poor, stupid, evangelical boy believed he HAD to go and share with them an alien message because in his THOUGHT they needed it, otherwise they would go to some hell or other, failing to realise that they have no shame for their nakedness and are among the remnants of some prelapsarian and thus, innocent peoples still extant; who need no "saving" as it were, and are, most likely, closer to God than he ever was or could have been.

5. It was the same with the Warao peoples who worshipped their god Naparima, naked on San Fernando Hill here until banned by the British in 1936.

6. In light of this incident Christians seriously need to rethink their stance on sin, shame, and salvation as currently conceived and commended. This Sentinelese situation is a wound to such an understanding. And I don't think we've grasped how debilitating that can be for Judaeo-Christian Western thought.

The yearning to bridge the revelatory experience outside of the specific Jewish revelation of the Old Testament, Dutch Reformed missiology professor, Pieter Holtrop remarks whether Reformed theology, *"...is able to take people seriously, people as they are, people already touched by grace. In other words does Reformed theology take the doctrine of creation seriously...or must we admit that the Calvinist doctrine of grace and redemption does not have anything to do with historic reality, other than plucking people out of this' realm of darkness'? It causes Andre Karamaga to question the widespread opinion, even within the mainline churches in Africa itself, that the African cultural/ religious inheritance, when seen in the light of the gospel, was only to show darkness. It makes him wonder whether Reformed theology may admit that God, as known by Christians in the West, already was and is known in Africa, far before the missionary movement started witnessing to God, that Africa has its special knowledge, as the Giver and source of Life, life-in-community."* (1). And Andre Karamaga, a theologian with the All Africa Conference of Churches, himself has this to say, *"Nonetheless, I remain convinced that priority should be given to the dialogue of African Christians with themselves, because, in actual fact, entering the church does not cancel most of the values in traditional religion, which is both religion and culture. These positive values have therefore to be put in the light of the gospel, so that every African Christian may be internally reconciled and feel thoroughly African and thoroughly Christian."* (2) Again Karamaga asks probing questions, *"What has Christ contributed to the issue of God in Africa? What is Christianity's original feature which may warrant a Christian missionary invitation to Muslims and to believers in traditional religion? How can individuals and communities accept the Christian message, when they are steeped in a past and a present fraught with another cultural and religious heritage (traditional religion)? What befalls that heritage when an African joins Christianity? In other words, to what extent does conversion to Christianity create a break with the past and present, and where does such a break lead?"* (3). Rappai J. Nedumpara's attitude is that one can be converted to Christianity on the basis of one's valid, non-Jewish religious heritage and revelation, and can contribute such insights towards the further enrichment of the Christian revelation as they find a natural fulfilment there; and all this without having to violently sever ties with the past or present as some are wont to make of the jealousy of Yahweh in the Old Testament or of Christ's lordship in the New. Nedumpara is a Roman Catholic convert from Hinduism, living in Canada. His desire to witness to his new found faith has led him to make an investigation of divine revelation that would confirm his earlier religious experience as a stepping stone to a fuller reality. He posits his theory in his short book, "Who is Jesus Christ? Christ in the Bible, Christ in the Vedas, Christ in the Qur'an." (4)

With the passage of time, notions of good and evil, sin and salvation, sacrifice and atonement, predestination and fate, resurrection of believers (and even of god dying and rising again yearly) and after-life, baptism communion, grace began to be developed. This was side by side with philosophical concepts on the interrelatedness of creation, the nature of God, good and evil, truth, justice and order, and of conscience being a guide to moral conduct and right action. Can we just simply dismiss all this because it outside the pale of Judaeo-Christian revelation and therefore, 'pagan'? Does it mean that they are thus demon-influenced because only ideas and concepts that come through the Bible are divinely inspired, as we have been taught to say? Yet the Bible is far from original in any of its ideas at all! But clearly shows commonality of thought patterns and process of revelation. Why then would the Bible validate 'pagan' astrologers, a twofold sin, to be able to accurately read the stars and determine the time, place and nature of Christ's birth; a phenomenon held in common with the births of Krishna and Mithras? Or why then would it use the common idea of a resurrected god in the plan of Christ's ministry? Is there anything, then, so intrinsically wrong with the resurrection occurring at the Passover, i.e. in Spring when all other fertility gods were said to rise again from the death of winter, and using bunnies to symbolise vitality of life or eggs for the new birth or egg-rolling as the stone that blocked the tomb being rolled away? Can anything then, be demonic about December 25th as a birth date for Jesus? How can it be said to belong to another god, if Yahweh controls all time? Is it not 'a day that the Lord has made' and should we not rejoice and be glad in it.' Psalm 118:24?

What Judaeo-Christian biblical witness has done, however, is to take all it encountered and attribute it to its God, Yahweh alone, making him and not human religious activity the source of life, rather than attempt to sift any good from perceived evil, lest it "root up the wheat with the tares also", and leaving all to the wise judgement of God on the last day, Matthew 13:24-30. W. G. Jordan remarks, *"We need to bear in mind all the time that we are dealing with the complicated story of human life and not with an abstract theology. The Mosaic period is not a blank space upon which a new revelation is written in a mechanical fashion; the Israelites do not come into an empty land free from history and destitute of customs. The new must relate itself to the old in the way of conflict or absorption. Different types of thought and different modes of worship meet and mingle, but the faith in Yahweh shows its originality and strength by its power to live and conquer... Ideas attached to lower gods and demons were transferred to Yahweh, and then the thoughts concerning his being and character received a fuller purification and enlargement. The higher stage does not completely displace the lower..."* (5)

The process of divine revelation takes place in time, space and history. Religion has been culturally adapted and has used the story forms of myth and legend to convey truths about nature and natural phenomena that can now be understood by scientific verification due to ever-growing advancements in technology. The most notable of these is the persecution of Galileo Galilei by the Mediaeval Church, for teaching that the earth and all planets revolved around the sun, rather than the Church's view (once held to be divinely inspired) that the earth was the centre of the universe. Which teaching Galileo was forced to recant if he wished to remain in communion with the church. T. F. Torrance writes, "Because Revelation meets us in the creaturely reality of our fallen world, it conceals Christ behind Proclamation and Sacrament as well as reveals him. It is of the nature of mystery manifest in the flesh." 1 Timothy 3:16, cf 3:9; Ephesians 1:9, 3:3f, 6:19; Colossians 1:26ff, 2:2, 4:3 etc. ...So long as we wait for the redemption of the body, therefore, we are forbidden to have a static condition in the Church...otherwise that in the mystery of a worldliness that is already under judgement." (6).

Writing about the encounter of Christianity with other faiths in India, particularly Hinduism, Rev. Dr. Henry S. Wilson of the Church of South India says, *"In the Roman Catholic experimental Indian Mass, a few such prayers from indoor scriptures have been included. The Commission on Liturgy of the Roman Catholic Church in India has also compiled a selection of readings from scriptures of other religions which could be read during Christian worship. This may sound syncretistic to some, but if all 'good' has its source in God and if we believe that it is our responsibility to see that no barriers are constructed between God and people, all cultural channels of communication should be kept open. We have enough examples in the Bible as to how the apostolic church encouraged and incorporated what was good in 'gentile' cultures/religions. If this heritage is abandoned, it will only impoverish Christianity."* (7).

In general Reformation churches do not appreciate or sometimes acknowledge the contribution of 'pagan' thought on early church formation of doctrine. The prevailing attitude seems to be influenced by the Augustinian / Calvinist teaching of the 'total depravity' of the human race and by extension, all nature, due to the Fall of Adam. It says that no one can will or do any good, and that any appearance of good is tainted by sin. In order to will and to do God's pleasure, he of his own pre-determinate will and foreknowledge has predestined or elected some to eternal salvation. It was traditionally taught as a corollary to this that the rest were predestined to damnation as they deserve, but this is now rejected in favour of saying that they are left to God's judgement as he sees fit. Within this chosen band of saved ones, called a covenant, God sheds his rays of divine revelation while others grope in darkness and under the influence of evil forces. Henry Wilson again makes the point, *"Christians of younger churches had difficulty in incorporating their own cultural patterns based on the fear that what was not already 'sanctified' by God as 'Christian' could not be brought into the church. Such elements belonged to the realm of evil and would eventually be destroyed by God. Today, this may sound very naive, but that was part of our heritage. Even today many Christians and a few churches retain this dichotomy between 'Christian' and 'non-Christian' cultures."* (8).

The classic Calvinist attitude can be found amid the scholarly work on Reformed liturgy by J. J. Von Allmen, late professor at the University of Neuchatel, Switzerland, *"We shall see that Christian worship suggests not only a judgment on, but also a forgiveness of non-Christian forms of worship... There is no transition, no ladder reaching from one to the other. There is a gulf...: Do not be mismated with unbelievers. For what partnership have righteousness and iniquity? Or what fellowship has light with darkness? What accord has Christ with Belial? Or what has a believer in common with an unbeliever...It is not a preliminary, provisional, preparatory truth; it is the contrary of the truth. And that is why the Christian cult by its celebration protests against what, in the world, is deeper, more mysterious and determinative, namely, the pagan cult." (8). For Von Allmen, this attitude, "...Is a principle which lies at the root of the Biblical doctrine of election and which gives the latter its missionary bearing..."* (10).

And, why are there so many things in common with extra-biblical religious witness and thought? The Roman Catholic papal encyclical, 'Ad Gentes', returns to the church's original position of mutual exchange, saying, *"The seed which is the word of God sprouts from the good ground watered by divine dew. From this ground the seed draws nourishing elements which it transforms and assimilates into itself. Finally it bears much fruit. Thus, in imitation of the plan of the Incarnation, the young Churches, rooted in Christ and built on the foundation of the apostles, take to themselves in a wonderful exchange all the riches of the nations which were given to Christ as an inheritance (Psalm 2:8). From the customs and traditions of their people, from their wisdom and their learning, from their arts and sciences, these Churches borrow all those things which can contribute to the glory of their Creator, the revelation of the Saviour's grace, or the proper arrangement of Christian life...In this way, under the light of the tradition of the universal Church, a fresh scrutiny will be brought to bear on the deeds and words which God has made known, which have been consigned to Sacred Scripture, and which have been unfolded by the Church Fathers and the teaching authority of the Church. Thus it will be more clearly seen in what ways faith can seek for understanding in the philosophy and wisdom of these peoples. A better view will be gained of how their customs, outlook on life, and social order can be reconciled with the manner of living taught by divine revelation. As a result avenues will be opened for a more profound adaptation in the whole area of Christian Life. Thanks to such a procedure, every appearance of syncretism and of false particularism can be excluded, and the Christian life can be accommodated to the genius and the dispositions of each culture."* (11). This would indeed seem to be in harmony with the position of Church Father and apologist, Justin Martyr, of whom it is said, *"He is one of the first to strive to reconcile Christianity and Hellenic thought, by asserting that while the Church has the complete truth there are truths of philosophy as well, which, because they are true, must be due to the working of the same 'Logos' who revealed all truth in his incarnate life, who is both the creative Word and (as the Stoics also taught) the Divine Reason. Hence arises Justin's one original contribution to Christian thought, the conception of the 'Spermatic Logos'. Before the coming of Christ men had been enabled to attain to bits and pieces of the truth through the possession of 'seeds' of the Divine Reason; at Christ's coming the whole 'Logos' took shape and was made man."* (12). Justin Martyr demonstrates a liberal attitude to 'pagan' thought and shows how the church of the second century sought to commend the faith to others of like interest and similar cultural background.

Churches of the Reformed / Protestant tradition may be said to have made Jesus Christ too final in their Mediaeval attempt at purity of Christian doctrine and worship. There was no concept of the communion of saints beyond a horizontal relationship among members of the church militant. It was a religion stripped and 'purified' of the 'elohim', with no saints, spirits, jumbies or communion of saints with the church triumphant. There was a general denial and lack of any appreciation of the 'Mysterious', only an insistence on obedience to the moral law without any warmth of soul or imagination. It is said of the Rev'd. Alexander Kennedy, pioneer Presbyterian missionary to Trinidad and founder of Greyfriars' Church in Port-of-Spain, that upon the arrival of the Protestant Madeiran refugees to the island in 1846, seeking refuge from persecution by the Roman Church,
they were welcomed to services at Greyfriars' but were disallowed communion until services could be held in their native Portuguese, so that they could understand the gospel with their minds. Kennedy's strict Calvinism precluded this, because faith comes by a literal hearing of the ear and mind, whereas a more catholic understanding would prefer that one's faith grasps with the heart and imagination first and then with the mind, as when the Mass was celebrated exclusively in Latin, then being a vastly unknown tongue. Against Kennedy's action, the Refugees protested vehemently, claiming

that they fully knew and understood in their minds as well as their hearts and their faith what the celebration meant and thus language was secondary, if of no point at all. Communion with Christ and his church was of ultimate concern no matter how attained. But Kennedy was adamant, and they were debarred from communion until a Portuguese minister could be procured some months later. In this regard Paul Tillich would say, *"The general criticism of the Roman Church by all Protestant groups was the exclusion of the prophetic self-criticism by the authoritarian system of the Church and the growth of the sacramental elements of faith over the moral-personal ones... The break (with Rome) also brought about a loss of Roman sacramentalism and the unity based on them. In consequence of this loss, Protestantism became more and more representative of the moral type of ultimate concern. In this way it lost not only the large number of ritual traditions in the Catholic churches but also a full understanding of the presence of the holy in sacramental and mystical experiences."* (14).

The church in the Caribbean knows about this intolerance only too well, having been a principal agent of Western European colonialist expansion from the 15th to the 20th centuries. In an attempt to re-evaluate its role in a post-colonial society and in the midst of an awareness of other living religions, where Christian triumphalism is giving way to post-modernism, the Caribbean Conference of Churches hosted a Consultation on Popular Religiosity in Lelydorp, Suriname, in May 1994. The main purpose was to begin a process of dialogue and engagement with other faith-based communities that has continued to the present day, and which would allow for more effective ministry to the total community, in view of sharing the divine plan of creating a new humanity, recognising that there are societal problems and colonial legacies that challenge everyone regardless of religion. In their effort to be conciliatory towards other religious communities and to remove the stigma and stain of Western triumphalist intolerance, the Consultation designed a public Statement of eleven points, *"...drawn from a broad spectrum of faiths, having shared respectfully and sensitively the basic tenets of these faiths."* (15). The first statement concerns this work, namely: *"recognise the equal dignity and rights of all cultures and traditions..."* (16). It appears that the Consultation went too far in conceding the basis of the Christian faith in its all out attempt to remove, this colonialist / triumphalist stigma of being the 'conqueror / invader's religion', and any notion of some kind of superiority of revelation or practice, making itself equal in these regards to other communities of faith.

Peter Wyatt of the United Church of Canada wonders whether the planting of the gospel in a culture that has not known God as found in the Bible, i.e. One, transcendent and requiring a unique mediatorial access to the divine, can make these historic scriptural convictions in any way. He asks, *"Does thanksgiving offered to the sun, moon and wind constitute a confusion of the Creator / creature relationship, or is it only the manifestation of a cultural distinctive, akin to the 'Canticle of the Sun' of Francis of Assisi? The gospel challenges as well as blesses human culture, and it is responsible to ask of both older and younger churches whether there is a distinction between syncretism and inculturation."* (17).

Amaladoss here, is seeking to develop an integral approach to considering God's self-revelation to humankind and of humanity's response in the order of re-creating God's original purpose of one humanity in him. He places eucharistic liturgy in its context as the 'people's work', 'laos ergon' / 'leitourgia'. This liturgy is not restricted to attendance at the Lord's Table but rooted also in daily life in community with all its divergent and convergent streams of existence. For him, this integrating or convergent movement, *"... will, be carried by symbols that are capable of certain polyvalence around a central core and whose concrete connotations are controlled by the context of usage. This is what makes possible not only common reading of scriptures, common prayer, common celebrations, etc., but also the use of other religio-cultural symbols in the self-expression of the word. At the level of symbols a 'both / and' perspective, in the Oriental fashion, is more valid than 'all / nothing' or 'yes / no'."* (18).

Accepting Christ can then mean that the idolatrous, the distorted, the misdirected and the unclear can all find in Jesus the fulfilment of their longings and expectations, yet whilst recognising that this revelation in Christ is in itself imperfect, provisional and eschatological. The similarity of the evolutions of religious thought across the globe, the cross-fertilisation involved in some parts put us all on the path of seekers after God. What matters is not where one is along the journey, before or after Christ, but the plain idea of just being on pilgrimage. We are all on pilgrimage together. Kyoung Jae Kim remarks with clarity, *"God enjoys and blesses the diversity of the created world and the feast of the gospel. Through the descent of the Holy Spirit on the day of Pentecost the diversity of race, culture and tradition was affirmed, and the unity in diversity experienced (Acts 2:1-13) Diverse cultures and religious traditions are not a stumbling block to God's mission, but rather a creative challenge and opportunity to experience God's infinitude and depth of the gospel."* (19). The Event of Jesus Christ was a once-for-all event in human history, and there would be no more need for continual yearly rituals of death and rebirth, or of human action controlling natural phenomena. His event was a definitive point in human history that brings together the divergent strands of revelation, and knowledge of God's activity on the stage of human history, both before and after, into a convergent integrity specifically aimed at a final or eschatological and culminating consummation in the glory of God. It is this once-for-all, total and all-embracing activity of God in the human event of his person and work that stands as his Unique and Fulfilling revelation to humankind for all time.

NOTES

1. Pieter Holtrop, Mission as Life -In-Community: A Biblical Reflection, published in Reformed World, theological journal of the World Alliance of Reformed Churches, Geneva Switzerland, Volume 42, No. 2 June 1992, pg. 35.
2. Andre Karamaga, Mission and Contextualization, ibid. pg. 56.
3. ibid. pp. 56, 57.
4. Rappai J. Nedumpara, Who Is Jesus Christ? Christ in the Bible, Christ in the Vedas, Christ in the Qur'an; published by Family Prayer Mission, Mississauga, Ont., Canada.
5. W. G. Jordan, The Religion of Israel pg. 81: Peake's Commentary on the Bible, Thomas Nelson and Sons Ltd. 1919.
6. T. F. Torrance, Royal Priesthood, chapter 4—The Priesthood of the Church pg. 73: Scottish Journal of Theology Occasional Papers No. 3 1955, Oliver and Boyd Ltd.
7. Henry S. Wilson, Worship and Culture, published in Reformed World, theological journal of the World Alliance of Reformed Churches, Geneva Switzerland, Volume 46, No. 1, March 1996, Volume 41, No. 2, June 1990, pg. 61.
8. ibid. pp. 59-60
9. J. Von Allmen, Worship Its Theology and Practice, Lutterworth Press, London, 1965; part 1: Problems of Principle, chapter 3, The cult, the end and the future of the world, section c, The Christian cult as the pardon and the fulfilment of non-Christian cults, pp. 75-76.
10. Ibid., Chapter 8, The time of the cult, section 3, The Sanctification of time, pg. 238. 9-60.
11. Papal encyclical, Ad Gentes, para. 22, quoted in Out of the Depths, a collection of papers presented at four Missiology

Conferences held in Antigua, Guyana, Jamaica and Trinidad, in 1975, ed. Idris Hamid, pp. 18-19.
12. The Early Christian Fathers, A selection from the writings of the Fathers from St. Clement of Rome to St. Athanasius, Oxford University Press, 1956/69, ed. Henry Bettenson, Introduction pg. 10.
13. Paul Tillich, The Dynamics of Faith, 1957, Harper and Brothers, New York, N. Y. USA., chapter 1, section 6, Faith and Community pp. 28-29 and chapter 6, The life of faith, section 1, Faith and Courage, pg. 101. Ibid. chapter 4, Types of Faith, section 4, The unity of the types of Faith, pg. 72.
14. At the Crossroads, African Caribbean Religion and Christianity, published by the Caribbean Conference of Churches, 1995, ed. Burton Sankeralli, Statement from the Consultation on Popular Religiosity, Introduction, pg. 203.
15. Ibid. statement no. 1, pg. 203.
16. Peter Wyatt, To live with respect in creation: A Canadian Perspective, published in Op. cit. no. 1, pg. 10. 1. Patricia Willey, Sing to God a New Song—Using the Past to Construct a Future, published in Reformed World, theological journal of the World Alliance of Reformed Churches, Geneva Switzerland, Volume 46, No. 1, March 1996, pg. 46.
17. Michael Amaladoss S. J., Culture and Dialogue, pg. 176.
18. Ibid.
19. Op. cit. no. 4. pg. 19. 4. Kyoung Jae Kim, A Northeast Asian Perspective (on Gospel and Cultures), published in Reformed World, theological journal of the World Alliance of Reformed Churches, Geneva Switzerland, Volume 46, No. 1, March 1996, pg.16

FIVE 'SOLAS', FIVE HUNDRED YEARS ON BEING A COMMEMORATIVE LECTURE TO MARK THE QUINCENTENARY OF THE PROTESTANT REFORMATION ON REFORMATION DAY / ALL HALLOWS' EVE, TUESDAY 31ST OCTOBER 2017 AT THE TRANQUILLITY METHODIST CHURCH, VICTORIA AVENUE, PORT-OF-SPAIN, TRINIDAD AND TOBAGO, WEST INDIES.

There can be no doubt in anyone's mind that the Protestant Reformation has vastly altered and influenced the Christian Church and the Western world. It opened the way to the development of much stronger ideas of the nation state and of the sphere and limits of the influence and control of the Church over the State. The availability of the Bible in the hands and language of the common people through the newly invented printing press allowed art, literature, and science to flourish.

But the Reformation is called, Protestant, not only because of an action against an establishment and a hierarchy, but out of a desire to 'testify to / pro testare' the authority and primacy of the scriptures of the Old and New Testaments. Martin Luther, a German Augustinian monk and scholar had discovered an awareness of God's grace in his reading of Paul's letter to the Romans and in his own religious order the resources of an Augustinian theology of grace that he wanted to apply to the wider church. Luther publicly protested on October 31, 1517, in his Ninety-Five Theses against the sale of indulgences. Simplifying a complex issue, indulgences were certificates of pardon authorised by the papacy that was thought could shorten the time suffered in purgatory by the buyer or his deceased relatives. Although indulgences continue to be offered by the Roman Church, it would be very hard to find even the most die-hard Roman Catholic who would now defend the horribly emotionally manipulative "indulgence preaching" of the Dominican friar Johann Tetzel, with his tasteless reassurances that anyone buying one of his indulgences would find mercy from God even if he had defiled the Virgin Mary. Only a degree less vulgar was Tetzel's reputed jingle "As soon as the coin in the money-box rings, a soul from purgatory springs!" When Luther and his fellow Reformers turned to Scripture as the church's sole infallible authority, they found in its pages the teaching that sinners are justified (accepted as righteous by God) through faith alone in Jesus Christ alone. This was the gospel of the Reformation.

Armed with these two principles—the sole infallible authority of Scripture and justification by faith alone in Christ alone—Reformers all over Europe cast off the dead weight of papal authority and reformed their existing churches, sometimes at the city level, as in Calvin's Geneva, and sometimes at the national level, as in Scotland under John Knox. In so doing they maintained that they were not forming any 'new' church but reforming the one Catholic Church according to scripture. Indeed, Ecclesia Anglicana and Ecclesia Scoticana, the Church of England and the Church of Scotland both steadfastly maintain the origins of their churches long before submission to Roman papal authority at the Synod of Whitby in the year 664, and its removal therefrom and reversion to independent status at the time of the Reformation. In this regard both churches and the daughters that followed from them, the Anglican and Presbyterian communions, as well as the ancient Church of Moravia, Luther's Kirche, and the Reformed Churches of Europe also maintain the apostolic validity of their ministerial orders and sacraments as continuing from before and thus not needing Roman validity nor approval.

However, Luther came after a long line of heroes who sought after the purity of the Christian gospel and a more faithful reading of and adherence to the witness of Scripture, and the desire to have the Bible available in the vulgar tongue of the people; men such as William Tyndale, John Wycliffe, John Hus, Erasmus among others.

And yet this adherence to the authority of scripture also acknowledged the authority of the church and its tradition, including creeds and confessions, but always as subordinate to, and only as they agree with the Scriptures.

R.C. Sproul is helpful in explaining that although tradition does not rule our interpretation, it does guide it (1). And Jason Helopoulos reminds us that tradition is necessary because it is impossible to turn to one passage or book of the Bible to define baptism, prayer, atonement, or any other doctrine but a creed or confession can detail what the entire Bible says collectively about a specific locus of theology (2). Therefore, where our traditions, creeds, and confessions disagree with the Scriptures, they are to be rejected; where they agree, we embrace them and count them as useful for our Christian lives. Understanding this distinction is of paramount importance to understanding a church that is reformed according to scripture.

Now this adherence to the authority of scripture in all matters of life and doctrine and the gospel of justification by faith have left us with what has been abbreviated as the Five 'Solas': sola scriptura—scripture alone, sola fide—faith alone, sola gratia—grace alone, solus Christus—Christ alone, and soli Deo Gloria—to God alone be glory.

How far can these be relevant to the church today? And how much can we insist upon them in the multi-everything landscape and context that is Trinidad and Tobago, and which, maybe for the exception of the Guyanas, is vastly different and heterogeneous unlike the other English-speaking Caribbean territories. In other words, what should be the place of the Bible among the scriptures of the Hindu and Islamic faiths particularly? What does it mean to preach justification by grace alone through faith alone in Christ alone, among people of other faiths who have become emboldened and resolute in their beliefs since our gaining independence? Do we evangelise as in times past and which is continued among evangelical churches by demonising everything outside the Judeo-Christian revelation? We know that we can no longer evangelise offering the church as a means of upward social mobility, except maybe in the teaching profession and seeking to get our children into performing primary and prestige secondary schools. These questions we shall seek to address this evening.

Does Sola Scriptura imply Scripture ONLY? I believe the full implications of divine revelation on the Church's world view have not been fully grasped by the Church itself, particularly by churches of the Protestant Reformation. What / who and where is the Word of God? When does revelation end, and who ends it; God or the church? Does it end with the closing of the canon of New Testament scripture, or with the Event of Jesus Christ? Where was the Word of God before the Old and New Testaments were written or canonised? The church has been the one to define its source of authority and the bounds thereof, and that the church has also acknowledged the authority of the first seven Ecumenical Councils of the undivided church with regard to the nature of God and of the second and third persons of the Trinity, particularly, seems to infer that revelation is ever unfolding and we are called to continually "test the spirits" 1 John 4:1-3.

An interesting example where a particular interpretation of Scripture conflicts with another tradition can be found in the context of the Creation narrative. The church takes the traditional position of the Fall of humankind and the entrance of sin and death into the world through the disobedience of the first human pair. The concomitant shame that Adam and Eve have over their nakedness and a desire to hide from God, then eventually cover themselves in his presence and in each other's presence is taken as referring to the effects of sin and shame at the commission thereof as being a barrier to pure relationships. However among the Amerindian tribes of the Caribbean and South America, a different situation occurs. Warao Indians from the Orinoco Delta of Venezuela up until the 1930's annually made their way through the streets of San Fernando in Trinidad to worship at their holy hill of Naparima. They made this procession naked, but the ladies of the town, as proper British subjects, being modest and ashamed of the nakedness of these people, would offer them clothing, which they wore but only as far as the foot of the hill. At which point they discarded the Western, Judaeo-Christian covering of shame, for they knew no such thing, and ascended the mountain naked and worshipped their god there, unashamedly naked. The biblical Creation narrative cannot, therefore, have universal appeal as the divinely inspired reason for the condition of the created order and of the human race in particular, because whilst nakedness spelt shame and sinfulness for one people, for another it knew no such connotation, and yet the latter also experienced death and the ravages of sin and an imperfect human nature. Being ashamed of one's nakedness must therefore be a cultural accretion that was given a theological meaning. And the Creation story could be summed up as an attempt at a theodicy, [an attempt to explain the presence of sin, evil and suffering], rather than any divinely revealed simple answer to the world's condition.

Therefore the finality of divine revelation for the church cannot be the canon of New Testament scripture, or even Sacred Tradition as this too is ever unfolding. Paul Tillich holds the view that any attempt at infallibility of a decision by a council or a bishop or a book tends to the exclusion of doubt in the realm of faith, making it static. This static faith without doubt is idolatrous since the element of doubt seeks only to confirm that it involves a risk to be taken against reason; which risk-taking he calls 'courage' (3). Henry S. Wilson writes, *"The Commission on Liturgy of the Roman Catholic Church in India has [also] compiled a selection of readings from scriptures of other religions which could be read during Christian worship. This may sound syncretistic to some, but if all 'good' has its source in God and if we believe that it is our responsibility to see that no barriers are constructed between God and people, all cultural channels of communication should be kept open. We have enough examples in the Bible as to how the apostolic church encouraged and incorporated what was good in 'gentile' cultures/religions. If this heritage is abandoned, it will only impoverish Christianity."* (4).

Thus Reformed Christianity must have the courage to take the risk and acknowledge that there is a difference between canon and revelation; that God has been speaking to all peoples in all ages; that they have received a measure of the truth; that the Bible is not the fulness or final repository of all divine revelation. It is precisely the church's present problem when it searches scripture to find answers to situations within modern contexts that are alien to the biblical landscape and timeline; as with divorce and remarriage, or the homosexuality debate. Some churches are consistent in regarding both of the above examples as 'sinful' and their practitioners as under the discipline of the organisation. Others accept the former but not the latter, and still there are those who accept the former and clamour for the latter. All of this is from scripture. And there are the age old debates about infant versus believers-only baptism, and Sabbath Day observance among others.

In this regard, Patricia Willey remarks, *"We admit now that the Bible is not one voice, not even a chorus, but a cacophony of claims and counter-claims. And just as two people stand further apart when they disagree, so the Bible's various voices create dialogical space among themselves that refuses to be reduced, no matter how much we moderns have tried to collapse its paradoxes together. In point of fact, it does seem to be modern people, not the writes or transmitters of scripture, who are troubled by this. Generations of forebears seem to have lived shamelessly untroubled by their authorization of a multi-voiced document that will not simply sit down and tell us what is what."* (5).

Reformation churches run the risk of being even more inconsistent when they confuse inspiration with divine revelation and the Word of God and then restrict them, with the life of faith and doctrine, to 'sola scriptura'. Hence the tendency to split into many-celled denominations and bodies, each at loggerheads with another over the "right" interpretation of scripture.

Furthermore, Reformation churches do not appreciate or sometimes acknowledge the contribution of 'pagan' thought on early church formation of doctrine. The prevailing attitude seems to be influenced by the Augustinian / Calvinist teaching of the 'total depravity' of the human race and by extension, all nature, due to the Fall of Adam. The classic Calvinist attitude can be found amid the scholarly work on Reformed liturgy by J. J. Von Allmen, *"We shall see that Christian worship suggests not only a judgment on, but also a forgiveness of non-Christian forms of worship… What accord has Christ with Belial? Or what has a believer in common with an unbeliever?"* (6). And Henry Wilson remarks concerning the 'dichotomy between

'Christian' and 'non-Christian', that the socio-political world order has found itself cleaving towards a seemingly inevitable cataclysmic clash of cosmic proportions between these two poles of religious fundamentalism, particularly in the response of the Right Wing to terrorist attacks in major cities around the world.

The Roman Church is not without its measure of criticism either. It too, acknowledges and maintains the dichotomy between Christianity and the 'others', although conceding that that the Jewish Old Testament faith is already a response to God's revelation, 'unlike other non-Christian religions'; and above all that in the Roman Church alone, the fulness of the Christian faith, doctrine, practice and experience and thus the fulness of the divine revelation, subsists (7). Paul Tillich comments on this apparent intolerance within these Christian polarities; the Roman Church's exclusive possession of the truth, on the one hand, and Protestantism's fundamentalist regard at all other forms of Christianity and religion in general, on the other. *"This situation which is the source of idolatry is also the source of intolerance. The one expression of the ultimate denies all other expressions. It becomes—almost inevitably—idolatrous and demonic. This has happened to all religions which take the concrete expression of their ultimate concern seriously."* (8).

The church in the Caribbean knows about this intolerance only too well, having been a principal agent of Western European colonialist expansion and Christian Triumphalism from the 15th to the 20th centuries. The Caribbean Conference of Churches' Consultation on Popular Religiosity in 1994 had as its main purpose to begin a process of dialogue and engagement with other faith-based communities that has continued to the present day, and which would allow for more effective ministry to the total community, in view of sharing the divine plan of creating a new humanity, recognising that there are societal problems and colonial legacies that challenge everyone regardless of religion. But it failed to acknowledge the uniqueness of the Church's missiological appeal, found primarily in Matthew's gospel 28:18, and again in Acts 4:12. This is the truth claim of Christianity, grace alone through faith alone in Christ alone. To surrender it would be to lose the raison d'etre of the Church, and to ask one to cease to be a Christian. Wolfhart Pannenberg does not view this as intolerance, but sees it as proclaiming the core of Christian inclusivism by being the source of the church's universal mission (9). Now because Christianity has a missiological mandate to proclaim an ultimate concern with Jesus as the Christ of God, the supreme and final revelation to humanity and by its prophetic voice to call into being the new humanity in him, it immediately negates an attitude of indifference, naturally begs an attitude of intolerance and triumphalism, but demands a spirit of humility, respect and forbearance since all, 'our knowledge is imperfect,' 1 Cor. 13:9, and again demands that we view human history and divine revelation sub specie christi. Why should one be a Christian and make such an appeal if Jesus were not the one saviour of humankind?

Without seeking to be indifferent and without adopting an attitude of intolerance and triumphalism we must ask, of what relation then, is Jesus Christ to the rest of divine revelation? Is he, as Karl Barth and Rudolph Bultmann see him as the Centre of human history? (10). Or, is he as for Donald Baillie, also the beginning and ending of human history? (11). Can we have a Christ without a christology? The question begs to be asked, if we all, then, worship the same God. How far can we understand the jealously of Yahweh in Exodus 20:1-7? A jealousy that has extended into Christianity with the exaltation of Jesus Christ as Lord, who alone has wrought salvation from sin and its consequences by his atoning, vicarious sacrificial death and mighty resurrection from the dead, triumphing over the powers of death and evil; the Christian Passover. Which jealousy has also led to the dangers of intolerance, triumphalism, and a theologia gloriae. Christianity must humble itself and discard these notions and put on rather the spirit of that love seen in 1 Corinthians 13, and avow Christ as harmoniser, fulfiller, Desire of the nations Hag. 2:6-7, the creator of the new humanity, Jn. 3:17, 4:39, 10:10b. Hence the Reformation maxim, "Ecclesia reformata semper reformanda!"

It is this vision of the new, re-created humanity that has prompted the church to be uniquely involved in a universal mission. The possibility of the new humanity has taken shape historically in the church with its various supporting ecclesiastical structures, and is meant only as a foretaste of the final reality. This is, as Henry Wilson understands the Christian vision, *"...the ultimate purpose of God, offering the possibility of a new community based on a new humanity made manifest in Jesus Christ."* (12). Many are the instances where the church has conveniently silenced its prophetic voice to call this new humanity into being. But because the gospel does not depend on the person preaching or the organisation commending it for its power, but from Christ who is himself the Messenger and the Message at once, then wherever it is preached it conveys Christ's grace and calls individuals into fellowship with God. Kyoung Jae Kim notes, *"Diverse cultures and religious traditions are not a stumbling block to God's mission, but rather a creative challenge and opportunity to experience God's infinitude and depth of the gospel."* (13).

The Christ Event was a definitive point in human history that brings together the divergent strands of revelation, and knowledge of God's activity on the stage of human history, both before and after, into a convergent integrity specifically aimed at a final or eschatological and culminating consummation in the glory of God. It is this once-for-all, total and all-embracing activity of God in the human event of his person and work that stands as his Unique and Fulfilling revelation to humankind for all time.

NOTES

1. 1. R. C. Sproul, The Agony of Deceit (editor), Baker Books 1997, pp. 34-35
2. Jason Helopoulos, https://tabletalkmagazine.com/posts/2017/10/is-scripture-alone-the-same-thing-as-scripture-only/
3. Paul Tillich, The Dynamics of Faith, 1957, Harper and Brothers, New York, N. Y. USA., chapter 1, section 6, Faith and Community pp. 28-29 and chapter 6, The life of faith, section 1, Faith and Courage, pg. 101.
4. Henry S. Wilson, Worship and Culture, published in Reformed World, theological journal of the World Alliance of Reformed Churches, Geneva Switzerland, Volume 41, No. 2, June 1990, pg. 61.
5. Patricia Willey, Sing to God a New Song—Using the Past to Construct a Future, published in ibid Volume 46, No. 1, March 1996, pg. 46.
6. J. J. Von Allmen, Worship Its Theology and Practice, Lutterworth Press, London, 1965; part 1: Problems of Principle, chapter 3, The cult, the end and the future of the world, section c, The Christian cult as the pardon and the fulfilment of non-Christian cults, pp. 75-76.
7. Geoffery Chapman, Catechism of the Catholic Church (c) 1994; part 2, chapter 3, article 9, paragraph 3, section 3, nos. 839-848, pp. 195-196, The Church and non-Christians and Outside the Church there is no salvation.
8. Op. cit. no. 3, chapter 6, The life of Faith, section 5, The encounter of Faith with faith, pg. 122.

9. Wolfhart Pannenberg, An Introduction to Systematic Theology, chapter 4—Christology within a Systematic Framework pg. 54: Wm. B. Eerdmans Publishing Co., Grand Rapids, Mich. USA, (c) 1991, reprinted 1992.
10. Donald Baillie, God was in Christ, An Essay on Incarnation and Atonement, Faber and Faber Ltd. London, 1956/63/68/73, chapter 3, Why a christology?, section3, Christology and the meaning of history, pg. 77.
11. Ibid. pg. 74
12. Henry S. Wilson, Reformed World, theological journal of the World Alliance of Reformed Churches, Geneva Switzerland, Volume 42, No. 2, June 1992, Introduction pg. 33.
13. Kyoung Jae Kim, A Northeast Asian Perspective (on Gospel and Cultures), published in op. cit. 4, Volume 46, No. 1, March 1996, pg. 19.

THE ETHIOPIAN EUNUCH: AN ESSAY ON GENDER IDENTITY

Deuteronomy 23:1 *No one whose testicles are crushed or whose penis is cut off shall be admitted to the assembly of the Lord.*

Acts 8:37 *As they were going along the road, they came to some water; and the eunuch said, "Look, here is water! What is to prevent me from being baptized?" 38 He commanded the chariot to stop, and both of them, Philip and the eunuch, went down into the water, and Philip baptized him. 39 When they came up out of the water, the Spirit of the Lord snatched Philip away; the eunuch saw him no more, and went on his way rejoicing.*

Matthew 19:11 *But he [Jesus] said to them, "Not everyone can accept this teaching, but only those to whom it is given. 12 For there are eunuchs who have been so from birth, and there are eunuchs who have been made eunuchs by others, and there are eunuchs who have made themselves eunuchs for the sake of the kingdom of heaven. Let anyone accept this who can."* Bible quotations taken from the New Revised Standard Version (NRSV)

At the beginning of December 2018 the Church of England issued a "Pastoral Guidance for use in conjunction with the Affirmation of Baptismal Faith in the context of gender transition", for its clergy on the manner in which transgender people should be welcomed into the Anglican faith using the 'rite of Affirmation of Baptismal Faith' as the key part of a service to recognise a person's gender transition. the advice states, *"The Church of England thus welcomes and encourages the unconditional affirmation of trans people, equally with all people, within the body of Christ, and rejoices in the diversity of that body into which all Christians have been baptized by one Spirit."* (1). In paragraph two of the statement of advice it states inter alia, *"The image of God, in which we are all made, transcends gender, race, and any other characteristic. Our shared identity as followers of Jesus is the unity which makes all one in Christ (Galatians 3.27–28)."* (2). Just over three years ago in July 2015, the Evangelical Lutheran Church of America ordained the Rev'd. Asher O'Callaghan as a pastor, making him the first transgendered person to receive holy orders in a Christian Church.

In the Bible we find this passage from Isaiah 56:3-6 New Revised Standard Version *"Do not let the foreigner joined to the Lord say, "The Lord will surely separate me from his people"; and do not let the eunuch say, "I am just a dry tree." 4 For thus says the Lord: To the eunuchs who keep my sabbaths, who choose the things that please me and hold fast my covenant, 5 I will give, in my house and within my walls, a monument and a name better than sons and daughters; I will give them an everlasting name that shall not be cut off."*

And in the New Testament in Acts 8:26-40, we read of the baptism of an Ethiopian Eunuch by Philip the Deacon and, according to tradition, his being the first Christian missionary to Africa, taking the Gospel to the "uttermost ends of the earth" after having gone from Jerusalem to Judea and Samaria from whence Philip came to baptise him. This was to follow the Lord's pattern of evangelism as he directed the apostles in Acts 1:8.

The word eunuch is defined by Ujwala Sunil Sindhe as coming from two Greek words, eune ("bed") and ekhein ("to keep"), effectively "bed keeper". They were found predominantly in older civilisations as castrated males who primarily guarded the ruler's harem of wives, their being incapable of sexual arousal. Many of them would develop effeminate qualities, having been castrated in early teenage years so as to preserve their youthfulness and unbroken voice, seeing that their bodies could not produce the testosterone needed to develop a commonly accepted form of masculinity. Cohabiting among the ladies of the court to guard them and serve them without any doubt, they were accepted as one of the group. Some eunuchs occupied higher and more respected positions at the imperial palace being employed to perform such domestic duties as making the ruler's bed, bathing him, cutting his hair, carrying him to his toilet, relaying messages as a trusted servant, and even serving as trusted advisors to the ruler. Eunuchs were generally not allowed to have loyalties to the military, the aristocracy, nor to a family of their own having neither offspring nor in-laws, at the very least, and were thus seen as more trustworthy and less interested in establishing a private 'dynasty' In India during the era of the Moghul Dynasty a number of high-status job openings became available for eunuchs. As a result, poor families often converted one of their sons into a eunuch and had him work at an imperial palace to create a steady source of revenue for the family and ensure a comfortable lifestyle for the son. Eunuchs were highly valued for their strength, ability to provide protection for ladies' palaces and trustworthiness. (3). Unlike most of the other nations in the Middle East, Judaism never condoned castration either as punishment or to produce a servant class of court functionaries. Indeed, castration was seen as a foreign practice, and scripture, speaking to the exiles, warned that their sons would "be made eunuchs in the palace of the king of Babylon" (Isa. 39:7; 2 Kings 20:18).

Eunuchs were considered a kind of third gender in the ancient world, considered a neuter gender in a manner of speaking, being effectively neutered as it were; having the appearance of being male with masculine genitalia but without the ability to reproduce sexually and possessing many feminine qualities owing to the absence of testosterone in the body. Eunuchs must not be confused with male / female transsexuals, who often choose to undergo a sexual transition, along with estrogen or testosterone therapies and other surgeries, to feminise or masculinise their bodies, as the case may be. It may be seen as a form of being transgender but particularly of emasculation moreso.

The LGBTQIA+ et al have not generally made such a choice to be who they are but have been born with such innate qualities of same sex attraction, but the Church has lost its welcoming aspect along the way and become as much closed as the Old Testament Jewish community. The Church has exalted virginity and celibacy as qualities of the Kingdom of God, equal to the virtue of marrying and procreating, against the Old Testament example. The Church has also encouraged a form of gender identity obscurity by having women cut their hair (their glory and beauty 1 Cor. 11:15), and take on masculine names such as Mother Dominic, Mother Francis and so on, in a form of blatant emasculation based upon an ancient Roman theory that a woman is an incomplete male.

Not being able to procreate children they were among those cut off from the covenant and the Temple worship of the Old Testament as decreed in Leviticus 21 and Deuteronomy 23:1ff. This was also extended to the self-hating of virginity and infertility among women, so that a barren woman prayed fervently for her "curse" to be removed and to conceive a child- Sarah, Hannah, Samson's mother, Elisabeth, et al. Jephthah's daughter in Judges 11:37ff wept as her father made a vow to give to the Lord the first thing he saw on returning home, if he were successful in battle. She had thus lost her womanhood to marry and have children. The baptised Ethiopian eunuch and others like him, found welcome in the Christian community despite their sexual orientation which was not distinctly male nor female. The eunuch made a wilful choice to transgender from male to neuter for the sake of a particular job requirement yet still found welcome among Christ's followers, and even became the first missionary and evangelist to the African continent! Some eunuchs in the nascent Christian world found place among the great theologians and philosophers such as Origen of Alexandria and Pierre Abelard, and several have even been canonised as with St. Ignatius of Constantinople.

Kathryn Ringrose posits the notion that the idea of angels in the Bible were modelled on the eunuchs of antiquity. Both eunuchs and angels have beardless faces and after the Great Flood of Genesis 6 and 7, when the "sons of God found the daughters of earth fair" and copulated with them creating a mutant race, angels became asexual and non-reproductive in Jewish lore. Yet still, we have come to assume that angels are masculine because of their reproductive power in the Genesis account, most probably, and have attributed their names in Scripture as being masculine, as with Michael, Gabriel and Raphael. God, though, is perceived as surrounding himself with angels as advisors and emissaries just as kings and emperors in antiquity were similarly surrounded by eunuch advisers and emissaries. (4)

Who ever said that angels were asexual, non-marrying and non-reproductive? Richard Joel Wassersug also writes, *"The liminal status of court eunuchs, who were neither males nor females, neither commoners nor kings, gave them a unique privilege, the privilege of passage through palace walls. This meant that they could on one hand mingle with the masses, while on the other, be free to enter the inner court (e.g., the Forbidden City in Beijing) and the most important sites of government. They both guarded the portals and were free to pass through them... Eunuchs inhabit a gender space that is partially male, partially female, but not completely either. In gender-segregated cultures, our in-betweenness allows us to be able to transgress both worlds. Eunuchs of antiquity could pass through literal and social walls and live in the world of both commoner and king. Being neither fully male nor fully female, they could also emotionally function in both gender terrains..."* (5)

In India there is the concept of the HIJRA, a eunuch associated with a deity and with certain rituals and festivals—notably the devotees of Yellammadevi, or jogappas, who are not castrated and the Ali of southern India, of whom at least some are (6). That the Judaeo-Christian experience is highly patriarchal is clearly recognised in the Bible. This apparently seems to be a feature of monotheism wherever it is found. God is given an ultra-maleness not found anywhere else in religious thinking except in the other great monotheistic religion of Islam, which is a stream from original Old Testament revelation, i.e. claiming its heritage from the line of Abraham. Even when Egypt under Pharaoh Akhenaten was forced into monotheistic adherence that God was confined to being male as, Aten. Traditional Christianity takes this concept even further when it insists on an all-male and mainly celibate clergy claiming that this was the original composition and eternal decree of Jesus for the church's ministry. And surprisingly, many of the other religions that would avow a feminine nature to the godhead, or plurality of gods, also strictly adhere to an all-male clerical priesthood; although there were priestesses and vestal virgins dedicated to ancient Greek and Roman goddesses. Thus there has always been a concomitant need to represent the divine in God's feminine nature.

But should a view of the nature of 'god-ness' acknowledged the world over be totally ignored by Judaeo-Christian religious experience? Can there be any truth to the contrary? Created MALE and FEMALE in his IMAGE and LIKENESS: therefore, if women were created in God's image and likeness, does that mean that God also has female qualities? The male which God shared with men and the female with women, and some who have a smattering of both to greater or lesser degrees? And we can also acknowledge that other middle ground where men do have a feminine side which in their "macho-ness" and sometimes toxic masculinity they are afraid to own up to, or taught by traditional trends to disavow, and women do have a masculine side which they are not ashamed to reveal.

In the Old Testament, the image of the Spirit brooding over the waters / formless waste, preparing the world for the creative word of God, Genesis 1:2, has been likened to a bird incubating its egg and awakening life. There is a reference to God's guiding the faithful, as a mother eagle caring for her young, Deuteronomy 32:11-12, and of God's vowing to comfort his own as a mother comforts her child, Isaiah 66:13. In the New Testament, Jesus describes his longing for the redemption of Jerusalem as a hen (not fowl-cock!) who gathers her brood under her wings, Matthew 23:27, Luke 13:34. And just as at the first creation when she, the Spirit, mothered all life and brought forth into being everything the Word was to say, so too she brings the new Creation into being by her divine activity in the Christ Event, and brings every new Christian to birth in the act of being born again. Are we going to ignore these altogether?

What does God mean when it is decided to create human beings in his own image, after his own likeness, Gen. 1:26? Is it of his own self, or does it include the "elohim" who as spirit beings may not be sexless then, but male and female, as rendered in the gods and goddesses of the other world religions? When we speak of God as 'Spirit" John 4:24, it is usually held to be in regard to genderlessness, and the references to maleness and femaleness, in regard to qualities of character.

The major absence of femininity in regard to God is seen by Evangelical Christianity as the reason for certain sections of the church exalting Mary, the Mother of Jesus, to a role that scripture does not render her explicitly; that of being co-redemptrix and co-mediatrix with Jesus because it was from her that he obtained his human nature, flesh and blood. And therefore, she is eternally united to him in a way that excludes all other human forms of communion with the divine, (7). And thus this desire for divine femininity is seen as a 'pagan' influence and outside of the biblical deposit of faith, not to be countenanced in their regard, and as such, the role of the Divine Mother needs to be recovered.

Hinduism is perhaps alone not in having separate male and female gods per se, but in seeing maleness and femaleness as complementary aspects of the Divine Being. Thus Shiva and Parvati, Durga, Kali, and Saraswati, or Vishnu and Lakshmi are male and female aspects of one god. Vishnu's incarnation as Ram has his female counterpart of Sita and as Krishna with Radha. And in many mantras these deities are invoked together, "Sitaram", or "Radhakrishna". It is not an attempt to make God in our image and likeness, which is idolatry and has regularly been used by monotheists of Hindus, but an attempt to recognise that earth reflects heaven in a Platonic way.

The prevailing world view of biblical times has, however, left us with the legacy of God as strictly male, Father and of a second God-Person as the Son who became incarnate as a male, and of the Holy Spirit described as 'He', Matthew 28:19, Luke. 1:32-35, John. 14:15, 15:26, 16:8-12. Modern feminist critique of the Bible would have us render the opening phrase of the Lord's Prayer as, *"Our Father/Mother"* (8), or the Trinity described as, *"Maker, Saviour and Spirit"* (9), or the Holy Spirit called the, *"Midwife of change and the new-birth"* (10). Modern trends, though, compel us to refer to God in the neuter gender, so as not to offend any group by using exclusively male or female terms or a mixture of both, but yet in so doing we may very well negate the qualities of his character with which we ourselves were created male and female.

Comparatively recent re-evaluation of the Old Testament has led biblical scholars to infer that the word for spirit in Hebrew is feminine gender, and the implication is that the Holy Spirit might be the feminine aspect of God, so long denied in a patriarchal world-view. But this could also mean that the generic word might be feminine gender but the thing described by that word might be another. For instance, in German there are three genders of words, masculine, feminine and neuter, rendered by the definite articles for the word 'the', as 'der', 'die' and 'das' respectively. The word for, 'the maiden', is, 'das madchen'. Here we see that although 'maiden' refers to an unmarried woman and therefore a female person, the actual generic word, 'madchen', is neuter gender with its definite article, 'das', and most probably because a maiden has not yet attained to full womanhood by the loss of one's virginity or maidenhead, and conception and delivery of a child, and thus is in a state of flux being neither male nor full female. Likewise the word for 'fire' in Latin, 'ignis', having its root in the Sanskrit, 'agni' is feminine in gender and so given feminine qualities, but is neuter by nature. Thus the gender of the generic word does not necessarily have any bearing on the gender of the thing or person described. So that 'spirit' in Hebrew may generically be feminine, but that does not necessarily say anything about the gender of the Spirit per se.

God's Spirit or Ruach, a feminine noun in Hebrew, took on a neuter form when it was translated into Greek as Pneuma. The Latin Vulgate of St. Jerome translated this as masculine Spiritus. God's Spirit, which at the beginning of creation brooded over the waters to bring forth abundant life, thus transcends all genders in the original biblical tongues. The Spirit brings forth life in the waters of Mary's womb at the New Creation in the Christ Event. A fascinating thought, therefore, would be that Mary was impregnated not by the masculine *Spiritus*, but by the sacred feminine *Ruach*, rather, two feminines, and not a masculine and a feminine to bring forth a "male" Jesus, as this would have been the gender in which she referred to the Spirit of God as Jew. The Bible is replete with images of the caring, consoling, healing aspects of divine activity. Because God as father has become a literalised metaphor, the symbol of God as mother is eclipsed. The problem lies not in the fact that male metaphors are used for God, but that they are used exclusively and literally. Images of God as female, which have been suppressed in official formulations and teachings as with the Creeds, in time came to be embodied in the figure of Mary who functioned to reveal the unfailing love of God and to fulfil the need for a feminine aspect in the Christian understanding of God.

The same problem arises with the gender of the Greek word for wisdom, 'sophia', which is feminine and to which a feminine quality has been ascribed in the Book of Proverbs chiefly. It has even become a woman's personal name in English. It has been revered as the feminine aspect of Jesus who is called the 'Word, Reason, Logos' of God which in Hebrew is translated, 'dabar' and which could have as its double meaning 'Wisdom'. The Jesus Seminar has sought, not only to ascribe this to Jesus, but moreso to worship 'Sophia' separately as a Christian goddess in itself. This would seem to be along the same lines as the cultic worship of 'Reason' and the religion of theo-philanthropy in France after the Revolution of 1789, and was condemned as heretical by the Church.

All this does not mean that the image of the Spirit portrayed as feminine is not beautiful or out of harmony with the Judaeo-Christian revelation. But in all things there must be balance and if the Spirit is to be truly like the wind, John 3:8, having total unconfined freedom to go wherever she wills, influence whomever she desires, or assume whatever shape or form she believes, then her feminine quality must be appreciated without injury to the male-dominated revelation, normally accepted as divinely inspired and the only image allowed in Christianity. When we do that (allow only male-dominated images for God) then we, more than all, become idolatrous, imagining and confining God to only one expression and seeking validation by claiming that it alone is divinely revealed. Thus we need also be true to the Biblical witness of the feminine images of God.

According to Count Zinzendorf, an early leader of the Moravian Church, the name which best communicates the reality of the Spirit's relationship to Christians is simply, Mother (11). Even as Jesus is referred to as husband in the writings of St. Bernard of Clairvaux, St. Teresa of Avila, and John Newton in his hymn, "How sweet the name of Jesus sounds'. In the latter's case there is a line which reads, *"Jesus, my Shepherd, Husband, Friend..."* but which in modern usage has the word, husband, rendered as, brother. And here is another type of relationship indeed, than the one originally intended by the writer. For if any Christian man has doubt as to whether it is politically correct to refer to Jesus as his husband, in spite of the trend towards recognising the equality of same-sex marriages, let him not doubt for a moment that as a member of the Church he is incorporated into the imagery of the Bride of Christ, which the Church as a unity is.

The acceptance of the third-gendered Ethiopian Eunuch into the New Covenant while being rejected from the Old begs us to look again at the first creation account in Genesis 1:27 where, *"[So] God created humankind in his image, in the image of God he created them; male and female he created them."* Is it possible that this could mean that the first humans were created gender-fluid / combined or transgender until separated as later in Genesis 2:21ff?

Are Intersex persons born with both male and female sexual organs, formerly termed Hermaphrodites, a result of sin and the fallenness of humanity when they were cast out of the Garden of Eden? This is the inheritance of St. Augustine of Hippo's doctrine of original sin that the church accepts as authoritative. Yet, there is another view found among the early church fathers such as St. Irenaeus that the world was not created perfect and fell from grace with humankind's disobedience. Rather, the world was created good, though not perfect, for if it were perfect then what was an evil tempter doing in the Garden of Eden? Thus the world was created to struggle and grow and develop from imperfectness to perfection, its ultimate destiny. Our human imperfections lead us into sin and destructive ways of living. The coming of Jesus Christ then seeks to renew the divine image within us, to take our inhumanity into himself on the Cross and disempower our depravity, and through his Spirit to live in us and do for us what we cannot achieve by ourselves, that is, to make truly human.

Some proponents of infant baptism baptise their children so as to remove this original sin inherited at conception. But are we indeed conceived in sin and born corrupt and depraved, as it were? This author undoubtedly practises and commends the doctrine of infant baptism but would prefer that such baptism be seen as an
affirmation of who we are created to be and to become, for we are always being

changed from glory into glory, 2 Cor. 3:18. It is an opening up of our lives to God's redeeming grace, and the leading and guiding of the Holy Spirit. Baptism, both infant and of believing adults, therefore recognises that we are heirs of grace and brothers and sisters of the Lord Jesus Christ, from our conception, destined for glory. It is an affirmation of being rather than being made into something we are not or which we do not have by nature, Psalm 139:13-16, Jer. 1:5. Thus to be baptised as an infant and then to grow and experience an aspect of gender fluidity whether naturally or having an inward sense that one's birthed body is not the one preferred to fully express one's gender, or whether one grows up to be any one of the letters in the LGBTQIA+ conglomeration is not a sin to be repented of but an identity that has already been affirmed along with all other human traits and characteristics via baptism, yielded to God to further mould us into what we were intrinsically designed to be according to his good and sovereign will and purpose.

There is need to acknowledge that the gospel transcends all cultures and that in any event, all cultures need the gospel. Reformed theologian Anne Hadfield, states, *"Our identity is in our baptism not our [physical human] birth. Our calling is to 'koinonia', an alternative community of genuine crosscultural fellowship in the face of increasing ethnic separation and violence. The community is not one where issues of domination or control are suppressed resulting in a false unity...Rather, reciprocity in this situation implies repentance for past injustices, and a reconciliation which ensures justice for all. Christians are called to be a sign of this vision where all are kin in the KINdom of God as they work as coworkers under the Lordship of Christ."* (12). To understand this call to koinonia and KIN-dom we must look again at Galatians 3:28, where, *"There is no longer Jew or Greek, there is no longer slave or free, there is no longer male and female; for all of you are one in Christ Jesus."* Here, Paul speaks to our universal salvation in Christ but also to our oneness in him, in his mystical body of which the Church is the visible and sacramental manifestation. Here, there are to be no divisions based on nationality, race, gender identity or social status. This is both a spiritual reality as well as a material experience. The kingdom of God for which we pray in the Lord's Prayer is one that breaks all human-made barriers. It is not only a future inheritance but must come on earth as it is in heaven. It is a radical political statement. It is Jesus' alternative to the Roman Empire. The kingdom is not the oppressive rule of earthly authority but a community of equals whose identity is rooted in their faith and loyalty to Jesus through their common baptism, through identification with the person and work of Christ, by removing those things that are foreign to justice, joy, mutual edification, compassion, peace, beauty, and order. Only in Christ is this oneness achieved when it transcends human categorical identity. The only human identity recognised is that of personhood, not whether you are male or female or eunuch or any other gender identification one may prefer, Jew or Greek, slave or free but rather what kind of person one is. In union with Christ, God makes us into the person GOD desires us to be, not what anyone else dictates or prescribes. This is why John Newton as a male can write, *"Jesus, my shepherd, HUSBAND, friend…"* The incarnate, risen, and ascended Jesus transcends all material human identities so that this quintessential human person can encompass and incorporate every soul into the eternal Self. From this true and fully human person flow our new and true personhood and identity and in communion with all who are so joined in and with Christ. And baptism cogently signifies and conveys this grace. Not for a moment must we doubt Paul's high sacramental theology when it comes to baptism.

Another provoking thought would seem to tend towards the notion of reincarnation, and although the author's Christian understanding of the nature of human and animal existence does not accommodate the generally accepted notion of reincarnation as found say in Hinduism, there is some sense of inhabiting a new body as promised in the doctrine of the resurrection. But what if there were some validity to the generally held view of reincarnation?If God is genderless then would not the soul created in his image also be genderless? Or if God is both male and female as Genesis 1:27 commends, then is the soul also limited to one gender defined by the body it inhabits in a particular lifetime? Say, for instance by reincarnation the soul inhabited a female body in one lifetime but in another it takes on a male one, would that not account for the increasing number of cases of gender-fluidity occurring in the world or coming to the fore in an ever-evolving human society; people seeking for a definite identity one way or the other, or choosing to remain fluid? It seems we will never know but it is nonetheless a fascinating concept! Humanity has always been evolving and perhaps it is taking on new and divergent ways of being and doing. After all was not Jesus born without any human male participation in his conception? Being described in John 1 as the "Logos" or eternal Word of God, this idea is related to the "Sophia" or Wisdom of God found in the Book of Proverbs and which is identified as feminine both in the Greek and the English renderings. Having been conceived of the effeminine 'Ruach Yahweh' and born of a woman with all his genes and DNA coming totally from a female, and being described as female in the Old Testament, in his pre-incarnate state as God eternal, and being found in the form of a human male in his incarnation, to all appearances, what would that make him then? Hmmm…

Honesty in the face of these exciting and fascinating biblical images can play a constructive role in challenging men, in particular, to be change agents in the face of HIV/AIDS, the LGBTQIA+ community, and gender-based violence, just to name a few. Men must be challenged to have new approaches towards power, confronting inherited toxic masculinities that have led them to consolidate such dominance based on intolerance, injustice, and inequity. This will require rigorous analyses of the religious, historical, and cultural factors that inform these aggressive masculinities. Deconstructing and reinterpreting these biblical texts must be undertaken in order to discover and deliver the justice men owe to all who have been swept aside, or had their voices silenced, or their humanity suppressed or robbed, whether by slavery, racism, colonialist subjugation, or commonly held patriarchal biases, prejudices, and doctrines of the headship of the male in some false view of a divine order; the sinned-against who long for redemption and the dignity to be fully human, in all that that humanity entails and the many and varied ways it has been created to be expressed.

For the sake of some religious stability we deny the evolutionary process in creation and human civilisation and development.

We concretise Christ in the Eucharist and deny his fluid mystical presence. We cast marriage into an unbreakable sacrament whilst acknowledging room for human error in every other aspect of life. T. F. Torrance reminds us, *"So long as we wait for the redemption of the body, therefore, we are forbidden to have a static condition in the Church…otherwise that in the mystery of a worldliness that is already under judgement."* (13).

What is the nature of the spiritual resurrection body that St. Paul speaks of in 1 Cor. 15, and of flesh and blood not being able to inherit the kingdom of heaven, 1 Cor. 15:50, especially in the light of humans in a new spirit body not having the gift of marriage? With no marriage, does it mean no sexual activity? That we may even cease to be strictly male and female in that regard? We need to take another, closer look at the doctrine of the ascension of Jesus who has entered heaven with our human nature, thereby uniting humanity with divinity and showing us the ultimate destiny of our humanity, perfected in the presence of God, Acts 1:9; 2:33; 7:56, Eph. 4:8-10. But also he continues to sympathise (feel, share, identify) with our human weakness and so be an able high priest and advocate representing us and our intercessions before God, Heb. 2:14-18; 4:14-16; 7:25-26. Dutch Reformed missiology professor, Pieter Holtrop remarks whether Reformed theology, *"…is able to take people seriously, people as they are, people already touched by grace. In other words does Reformed theology take the doctrine of creation seriously… or must we admit that the Calvinist doctrine of grace and redemption does not have anything to do with historic reality, other than plucking people out of this 'realm of darkness'?* (14). Jack Rogers thus argues that, *"The fact that the first Gentile convert to Christianity is from a sexual minority and a different race, ethnicity and nationality together calls Christians to be radically inclusive and welcoming."* (15)

Gender fluidity has always been with us though many in today's world refuse to see because of wanting to maintain an understanding of scripture the ancients never had. There are women who have more chest hair and can grow fuller beards than many men can. They have deep, masculine-sounding voices and are strapped in stature as any muscular man, and we are wont to call them 'butch' and Lesbian. There are many slender built men with no beards and even high-pitched voices who are apt to being called effeminate and 'sissy'. There are women with large breasts and women with tiny to indistinguishable ones. Some lactate on giving birth, others never at all. Male and female reproductive organs come in varying sizes, and some humans are born with both. These may be seen as accidents of birth and the gene pool, as it were. The Religious Right would, however, want to ascribe these and others to the effects of the Fall of humankind as a result of Adam and Eve's disobedience in the Garden of Eden, and thus, human identity in and of itself is regarded as intrinsically sinful and evil rather than sharing in the rich biodiversity of God creation that was created good and very good. So that to narrow the Creation narratives in Genesis to strictly male and female as if they came in uniform sizes and characteristics is to be dishonest with the nature of scripture. Much more can be said of the restrictions on inter-species breeding as per Leviticus 19:19 whereby humans could create a neuter animal such as a mule or a plant as a starch mango tree, not being able to reproduce their own kind of themselves. It was felt that this would extend to the races of humankind as interbreeding between a Caucasian and an African produces one who is called a 'mulatto' after the word mule. Thus even interracial marriage was forbidden on biblical grounds, as also with Ezra's admonition to Jews who had married Babylonian and Persian wives to divorce them, their mixed race making them become known as the hated Samaritans of New Testament times. Concomitant is the notion that any sexual activity that does not lead or open itself up to the procreation of children is somehow disordered, as with St. Augustine, who surmises that marriage is good but continence is better, and that sex only for pleasure, even in marriage, is a venial sin (16).

The Bible is not a book on biology or anything scientific; it is salvation history, and we must treat it as such. Revelation is sacramental in that it is conformed to time and history and uses earthly knowledge to portray heavenly truths, though imperfectly and naturally so. The earth and as such, the church on earth, can never reflect heaven in any Platonic way, but only dimly echo its sounds and forms. The revelations of the earth are essentially fragmentary and imperfect. All we have are broken snatches and glimpses of the Reality. Our revelation is therefore, eschatological, waiting for the dawning of the perfect day when Christ and the kingdom of God are revealed in all awaited and anticipated fulness.

NOTES

1. The Church of England "Pastoral Guidance for use in conjunction with the Affirmation of Baptismal Faith in the context of gender transition", December 2018
2. ibid.
3. Ujwala Sunil Sindhe, GENDER JUSTICE AND STATUS OF EUNUCH, International Journal of Humanities and Social Science Invention ISSN (Online): 2319–7722, ISSN (Print): 2319–7714 www.ijhssi.org Volume 1 Issue 1 ‖ December. 2012 ‖ PP.01-06. http://www.ijhssi.org/papers/v1%281%29/Version2/A110106.pdf?fbclid=IwAR0OBWUr5rtho6vaCimwqO4w8hk-O7F0A5aNSWiil97-vztI04ndOarQpQM
4. Kathryn M. Ringrose, The Perfect Servant: Eunuchs and the Social Construction of Gender in Byzantium, University of Chicago 2003
5. Richard Joel Wassersug, Embracing a Eunuch Identity, February 24, 2012, https://www.tikkun.org/newsite/embracing-a-eunuch-identity?fbclid=IwAR2Sxfr4nbAOSvaft_ePpIjRZRCTyPtxIppIVATz3IB6Wrf0pMzYJlwGCAU
6. Op Cit. no. 3
7. Geoffrey Chapman, Catechism of the Catholic Church 1994; chapter 3, article 9, paragraph 6, section 1, nos. 969-970.
8. J. Baker, D. Gay, J. Brown, Alternative Worship, SPCK 2003, pt. 4, Pentecost, pg. 111, The Lord's Prayer.
9. ibid. pt. 3, Easter, pp. 81/2 Jesus in the City.
10. The Church of Scotland, Book of Common Order, St. Andrew Press, Edinburgh (c) 1994, section 4, Prayers for the seasons of the Christian Year, pg. 443, Pentecost 1.

11. Dr. Craig D. Atwood, Zinzendorf and the Holy Spirit, Salem College—http://www.zinzendorf.com/atwood.htm
12. Anne Hadfield, A Perspective from the Pacific, published in Reformed World, theological journal of the World Alliance of Reformed Churches, Geneva, Switzerland, Volume 46, No. 1, March 1996, pg.35.
13. T. F. Torrance, Royal Priesthood, chapter 4—The Priesthood of the Church pg. 73: Scottish Journal of Theology Occasional Papers No. 3 1955, Oliver and Boyd Ltd.
14. Pieter Holtrop, Mission as Life-In-Community: A Biblical Reflection, published in Reformed World, theological journal of the World Communion of Reformed Churches, Geneva Switzerland, Volume 42, No. 2 June 1992, pg. 35.
15. Jack Rogers, Jesus, the Bible, and Homosexuality, John Knox Press, Westminster 2009.
16. St. Augustine, De Bono Coniugalis

ABOUT THE AUTHOR

The Reverend Clifford Reinhold Leandro Rawlins was ordained by the Presbytery of Guyana on behalf of the Church of Scotland in Trinidad in 1997, and served the latter as Associate Minister until 2005. He is currently the Minister of the Diego Martin United Church, the only fully ecumenical congregation in Trinidad and Tobago, founded in 1969 by the Methodist, Moravian, and Presbyterian Churches with assistance from the then Lutheran Church in America.

He holds a Diploma in Religious Studies (Cambridge UK) and a Licentiate in Theology (St. Andrew's Theological College, Trinidad), and is also a past National Music Festival winner.

He has taught Biblical and Systematic Theology with the Codrington College (Anglican Seminary, Barbados), Diploma in Theological Studies, Trinidad Campus since 2003, and is a founding and governing member of the Sehon Goodridge Theological Society. He also taught English as a Foreign Language for a number of years.

In 2006 he won the 2nd prize in the Georges Lombard International Essay Competition by the World Communion of Reformed Churches, on the theme: Water, source of life: socio-economic, theological, and interreligious perspectives. Then General Secretary Rev'd. Dr. Setri Nyomi noted, "There is great reason for optimism in our churches if this is the kind of scholarship that is taking place... The young theologians have reflected critically and creatively, putting their insights on theology and economics together in order to contribute to the emergence of a better world."

www.ingramcontent.com/pod-product-compliance
Lightning Source LLC
LaVergne TN
LVHW041851070526
838199LV00045BB/1547